Tugging
on
God's Hand

Other books by Penny Estes Wheeler:
    The Appearing
    Because You Prayed
    Longing for Home

To order, call 1-800-765-6955.

Visit us at www.reviewandherald.com for information on other
Review and Herald® products.

Penny Estes Wheeler, Editor

Tugging
on
God's Hand

Stories
You Love
from
Women of Spirit

REVIEW AND HERALD® PUBLISHING ASSOCIATION
HAGERSTOWN, MD 21740

The authors assume full responsibility for the accuracy of all facts and quotations as cited
in this book.

This book was
Edited by Penny Estes Wheeler
Designed by Tina Ivany
Electronic makeup by Shirley M. Bolivar
Cover photo by Kevin Morris/GettyImages
Typeset: 11/14 Goudy Old Style

PRINTED IN U.S.A.

07 06 05 04 03   5 4 3 2 1

R&H Cataloging Service
Wheeler, Penny Estes, 1943-   , ed.
    Tugging on God's heart: stories you love from *Women of Spirit*.

    1. Christian life.   2. Religious life.
I. Women of Spirit.   II. Title.

                248.4

ISBN 0-8280-1764-6

Dedicated to our authors.
Thank you for blessing our lives.

Contents

Introduction

Twelve years ago two women sat in my editorial office and shared their dream of a women's magazine published by the Seventh-day Adventist Church. A magazine written by women, for women.

"Impossible," I told them. "It will never happen."

So much for my short career as a prophet!

Women of Spirit made its debut in the spring of 1995. From its first issue it dealt with the nitty-gritty that makes up the lives of Christian women living and loving in today's complicated world.

These few stories are *not* the best of the best. Many, many more—just as engaging, just as encouraging and inspiring—did not make the final cut. We simply didn't have enough room. That's too bad, but in a way it's good. If you like this one, there's another book just waiting to be published. And, of course, *Women of Spirit* is bringing you brand-new stories every two months, all year long.

May God bless as you share in the lives and stories of your sisters from around the world.

—Penny Estes Wheeler, editor
Women of Spirit
www.womenofspirit.com

Tugging on God's Hand

Gloria Carby

She stood in the shelter of the little red playhouse shedding silent tears. Her mom had just said goodbye for the day, leaving her at the day-care center.

I invited 2-year-old Sarah to go for a walk around the play yard. As I held her tiny hand I sang, "Shall we go for a walk today and see what God has made?" We stopped now and then to identify different things "God had made," such as flowers and leaves of a tree.

Each morning after that Sarah came to me and tugged on my hand, indicating that she was ready for her walk.

Today, two years later, as I entered the play yard my eyes rested on 2-year-old Nichole standing in the shelter of the little red playhouse. Silent tears fell from her eyes. I started toward her, but before I could reach her Sarah walked up to her and took her hand. With a little smile she led Nichole on a walk, singing, "Shall we go for a walk today and see what God has made?"

Today it is I who stand in the shelter of the little red playhouse shedding silent tears. And in my mind I slip my hand into God's hand and ask Him to walk with me.

~ ~ ~

Gloria Carby is director of the Kingsway College early childhood center in Oshawa, Ontario. Gloria works with women's ministries in her conference. She and her husband, Robin, live in Bowmanville, Ontario.

Grandma's Pear Tree

Jo Anne Chitwood Nowack

I loved my grandma. I want to establish that right from the start, because I wasn't always the most respectful kid in the world. Sometimes I didn't understand her ways.

"Alyson," she might say one morning when she could plainly see that I was curled up in the window seat totally absorbed in a Don Coldsmith Western. The cowboy might be just about to kiss the girl, but that wouldn't matter to her. "Alyson," she'd repeat, just a little more forcefully this time. "Honey, I want you to take this loaf of bread over to Mary Jones. She's been sick, and I know she hasn't been strong enough to bake." She'd wipe her hands on her apron and get "that look" in her eye. When she got "that look," I knew that the cowboy was going to have to kiss his girl some other day.

"If you don't mind, while you're there, could you wash up her dishes and see if her floor needs mopping? She might need to have some laundry done, too."

Grandma would get this pleased look on her face as she swaddled the loaf of bread. She seemed happy to have fresh bread and an able-bodied granddaughter to deliver it in love to a friend in need. I'd often heard her say that there was more religion in a loaf of bread than in 10 sermons. I wasn't sure how much religion there was in me, but that didn't seem to matter to Grandma. She offered me anyway. That's the way she was—practical about her religion. It could be very inconvenient at times.

I would sigh dramatically as I plopped my book down, and mutter under my breath (rather disrespectfully) about never having a life of my own. Grandma would give me a long, sideways glance, but that was all.

I always ended up feeling good about what I'd done after I'd finished running Grandma's little "love errands." I usually forgot all about the book I'd been reading long before I got home. It's a good thing, too, because Grandma invariably had come up with a job or two of her own that she needed "a spare pair of hands" to accomplish.

As much as I grumbled and complained about having to help her, the truth of the matter is that I actually enjoyed it. I tried not to let it show too much for fear Grandma would increase my pleasure by giving me more work to do. (A masochist I'm not.)

Grandma's kitchen was a wonderful potpourri of scents, sights, and tastes. Warm bread fresh from the oven. Strawberry jam cooling *rich* red in jars with checkered tops. Pastry crust sprinkled with cinnamon and sugar, and baked until it was light and crispy enough to melt on your tongue. I loved her kitchen. Especially at canning time.

To Grandma, canning was a spiritual experience. The process began when the garden was tilled in the spring and the first seeds of life were sprinkled into the cold black earth. It ended with row after row of Mason jars lined up in regiments of tomato red, blue lake green, and apricot orange, waiting to march onto Grandma's table and be consumed with a thick slab of homemade bread.

Canning represented the culmination of the life cycle. It was the goodness of God sealed up in a glass with a metal lid. It was a sacred task that she and I both took very seriously. But probably for different reasons.

Grandma prided herself in growing everything she needed for the summer's canning on her own place. The old apple tree by the far pond yielded more than enough apples for a winter's supply of sauce and butter. The garden produced squash, tomatoes, beans, and potatoes. It grew onions and peppers for salsa and cucumbers for pickles. Herbs grew in sturdy clumps by the back door, and a rhubarb patch elbowed its way into the south end of the garden every year, invited or not.

But Grandma's uncontested pride and joy was the pear tree that grew behind the goat shed. It was magnificent to behold, and yielded a good six shelves of glistening white canned pears with enough left over to share with several neighbors. Grandma called it "my pear tree" with the same affectionate quality in her voice that you would expect to hear in reference to a favorite son.

At this moment the pear tree was in full glorious bloom, and Grandma's bright-blue eyes shone in anticipation of the fruit to come. We had had an unseasonably mild spring, even for Tennessee, and every green thing on the place seemed to vibrate with the warmth of the spring sun.

It was late afternoon when I noticed a cold wind blowing in from the north. Grandma pulled a sweater around her shoulders and glanced anxiously at the northern sky. "They said it was going to freeze tonight, but I didn't believe them. Why, it's nearly the middle of May!"

The temperature plummeted, and Grandma and I busied ourselves covering squash, bean, and tomato plants to protect them from the frost. It was almost dark when we finished.

Grandma straightened and brushed away a stray lock of silver hair from her face. "That's all we can do," she said, staring to the east. "The rest is in the Lord's hands."

I followed her gaze to the magnificent pear tree, and I was slapped by the realization that there might not be any pears this year. I could tell the same thought was beating on Grandma, too, judging by the tears that welled up in her eyes. I put my hand in her apron pocket, as I used to do when I was a little girl and wanted to be close to her, and we walked back to the house in silence.

"Alyson," Grandma said quietly as I was slipping away to my room that night, ready to go to bed. "Alyson, come pray with me for the pear tree."

I stared at her, waiting for her straight face to crack and a twinkle to break through from behind her eyes the way it did when she was pulling my leg and couldn't hide it any longer.

"What?" I began to wonder if the exertion of covering the garden plants had taken its toll on Grandma. But she didn't look tired. And the expression in her eyes was deadly serious.

"God knows how much that tree means to me. To us. I'm going to ask Him to protect it from the frost. I want you to join me. Will you?"

Of course there was no way I could refuse a request like that. I knelt by the kitchen table and listened in awe as Grandma had a discussion with God about her pear tree and the importance of this year's crop to her pantry. I had the feeling that if I opened my eyes, I'd see God sitting in one of her old oak chairs. I didn't want to risk it, so I kept them shut tight.

Grandma's face was serene as she kissed me good night. I slipped into bed wondering how God was going to save the pear tree. I'd read in magazines about how orange growers in Florida run huge fans to keep the air stirring and thus prevent the frost from settling on the fragile blossoms. I was still wondering about it as I drifted off to sleep.

I was awakened by someone shaking me vigorously. I blinked the sleep out of my eyes enough to see the halo of silver hair framing a shining face.

"Alyson, you *must* get up right now and come with me." Grandma didn't wait for me to pull on my jeans, but hurried down the stairs and out the back door. I leaped from my bed and raced to catch up with her. I'd never seen her so excited.

One peek out the back door revealed a world visibly altered by Jack Frost's white brush. Delicate frost patterns laced the windows of the goatshed. The morning sun cast a peach-colored glow over the landscape, already melting the frost here and there. Whatever damage was done had occurred just before sunrise.

A strange low hum filled the air. Grandma took off across the backyard toward the goatshed, slippers and bathrobe flying. I pounded right on her heels. When we reached the pear tree, the sound grew louder. The pear blossoms seemed alive, moving and humming like a thousand bees.

I looked closer. There *were* bees! Each bee was positioned in front of a blossom fanning the flower with its wings for all it was worth.

A few minutes later all the bees were gone. The temperature had risen above freezing, and the pear blossoms were no longer in danger. Grandma was laughing and crying and hugging me all at the same time.

I stood in shock. I looked back at Grandma and back at the beautiful flowering tree, then back at Grandma. By now she was on her knees, thanking God for saving her pears. I looked around half expecting to hear Him say, "You're welcome."

Grandma is gone now. She died last year of cancer. She died at home with the family all gathered around her, praying with her, singing her favorite old hymns, and telling her how much they loved her and would miss her. She died with a smile on her face, no doubt knowing that the next face she'd see would be that of an old Friend, and they'd laugh about the pear tree and the little bee helpers that fanned the frost away. He'd tell her secrets about her life that she'd only guessed, and together they'd plan to can a few jars of fruit from the tree of life.

~ ~ ~

Alyson told this true story to JoAnne Nowack, a hospice nurse, who was caring for her grandmother. JoAnne and her husband, David, live in Montana.

Fourteenth Palm Tree Down

Elizabeth Boyd

It was the last day of school. It was our last English class. Mrs. Smith closed the book and looked at us silently for a moment, then began to speak. "This is the last time we'll all be together like this," she began. "I've grown fond of you. You are very dear to me. And," she continued, "I want to make an appointment with you."

We listened, wondering what she meant. "Things will be very busy that first Sabbath when we get to heaven. There'll be reunions of all kinds. There'll be the tree of life to see, lost loved ones to find, our new homes to see. So it's on the second Sabbath that I want to meet you there.

Silver street

"There is a golden street there in heaven. And if there's a golden street, there must be a silver one, too. I like to think that they intersect and that Jesus has planted palm trees along the silver street.

"Now, everyone will be making appointments around the tree of life, but I want to meet you, along with all the students who have ever been in my classes, under the fourteenth palm tree down on the silver street on the second Sabbath right after worship."

Our thoughts were shattered by the closing bell. Our paths took different directions.

My path took me teaching.

It was the last class of my first year teaching. I closed the book. The class was silent, and then I began. "This is the last time we'll all be together like this," I said. And I told them about my appointment with Mrs. Smith, and we made our own appointment. We'll meet not far from Mrs. Smith's classes there on the silver street on the second Sabbath in heaven.

Our thoughts were shattered by the closing bell. Our paths took different directions.

Appointment renewed

A few years later I was walking down the corridor of a hospital when a familiar face, whose name I couldn't recall, came toward me with outstretched arms.

"Oh, Miss Elizabeth, Miss Elizabeth! Remember me? I was in your class your first year at Columbia Union College. Do you remember our appointment on the silver street on the second Sabbath?"

She was excited. "I've been telling my students about it, and we are planning to meet near your classes there on the second Sabbath."

Our paths took different directions again.

But the story doesn't end here!

You're welcome

Now, settled snugly in my church home in New England, I've been blessed with the earliteen division over a number of years. On the last class before they graduate from the eighth grade and into the youth department, we close our books and get out the play-dough. We build our own heaven. Each one makes their own personal contribution to the entire scene.

Then we make our plans for our own unique earliteen class reunion. And so the story goes on year after year with each class. My guardian angel is keeping my appointment book!

Our thoughts are shattered by the closing bell. Our lives take different directions.

But when they come home they meet me in the church corridor with open arms.

"Oh, Miss Elizabeth! Oh, Miss Elizabeth! Remember our appointment!"

Our lives take different paths.

It won't be long now and we'll be meeting with Mrs. Smith under the fourteenth palm tree down on the silver street. You'd be welcome, I'm sure. Just tell Mrs. Smith that Miss Elizabeth invited you.

~ ~ ~

Elizabeth Boyd, the founder of a nationwide traveling therapist registry, is an active mentor of teens in prayer and Bible study. She lives in a wonderful old farmhouse in Brunswick, Maine.

The Music Box
A personal story of abuse and recovery

Nicole Petersen

It came in a softly wrapped package, delivered with great care. The Maker had fashioned it lovingly, a gift for the ones who received it. Every tiny part of the music box had been crafted by skilled, experienced hands. Only the Maker knew the secret of creating within the little box a living, feeling heart that possessed the ability to learn, to turn experience into music.

But the recipients of this very special gift had no idea of the treasure they possessed. When they lifted the lid to hear the music, a plain, simple melody emerged, not so very different from that of other music boxes. In fact, its childish, faltering notes seemed inferior when compared to more elaborate boxes. This little trinket in their hands was just a plain, simple box that played plain, simple music. And so they carelessly cast their gift aside.

Time passed, and the heart inside the little music box ached to play its simple song. Instead it lived in a place filled with loud, raucous music, a place often full of violence, and the little box was often roughly knocked from its place. And every time it fell against the floor or wall, its lid cracked open and the plain, simple melody drifted out into the room.

But a loud, discordant sound drowned out the simple melody, and before it had a chance to finish, someone always slammed the lid shut and thumped it back into its place. So often was the little music box knocked about that its case became gouged and broken. Finally, in a fit of rage, someone picked it up and hurled it across the room. It lay on the floor in pieces, still trying to play its simple tune. But its notes were distorted and off-key. The other music blared and jangled all the louder, overpowering the feeble notes drifting from the damaged little box. After that, the family no longer wanted to be bothered with the broken trinket, so they threw it into the trash bin.

And then the music stopped.

The little music box lay buried under a heap of rubbish, trying and trying to play its simple song. But no sound would come out, because the living, feeling heart that the Craftsman had created in it was broken in two. It tried in vain to play the song of its Master Craftsman, but it had no music left in it now. So all it could do was lie there silently, its broken heart aching for the touch of its Creator.

But the Master Craftsman knew just where to find the precious, broken music box. He sent His apprentice to the exact spot it was buried, and the obedient helper gathered all the broken pieces together and brought them back to the Master Craftsman. To the apprentice's untrained eye the music box seemed beyond repair. He voiced his opinion to his Master, but the Creator merely took the pieces into His capable hands. He smoothed away the slime and grime from the trash bin, washing it with His own tears. He fitted the broken pieces back together and filled in the parts that were missing. He took great care and much time in repairing the broken music box, for it was of great value to Him. And at the end of each day He placed it in the middle of His workbench and propped the lid open.

The broken heart of the little music box rested in the safety of the Master Craftsman's workshop. And the more it rested, the more it healed, until one day a feeble little note—no louder than a sigh—emerged from deep inside it. So soft and faint was the feeble note that the apprentice didn't hear it. But the Creator heard, and turned with great joy and anticipation to pick up the music box and cradle it in His strong hands. The apprentice stood nearby, bewildered at His excitement. But before he could speak, the Master Craftsman said, "Be silent and listen. It is about to tell us its story."

The wounded heart rallied at the Master's touch. Weakly at first, then steadily stronger, the Creator's song flowed from deep inside the little music box. It sang its story, beginning at the point where it had first been unwrapped. It played a simple, faltering little song, stopping at every point where it had been interrupted before. And every time the song of the Creator stopped, the loud, violent music of the home where it had lived took over. Tears filled the eyes of the Master Craftsman, for He understood the language of music, and He knew what the wounded heart was saying. All of the pain came bounding out of its still-hurting heart, and the Master Craftsman listened patiently, cradling the little music box in His hands. The angry, violent music grew louder and louder until it pounded and screeched through the room, echoing until the apprentice had to cover his ears. And then there was silence.

The Master Craftsman held the little music box to His heart, tears flowing down His cheeks. The pain from the wounded heart flowed into the Creator's heart, and for a moment the two hearts became one. And then a new, incredibly sad song began to flow out from the two hearts. And when the mournful music ended, the Master Craftsman set the little music box on His workbench once again, propping the lid open, lest the music should stop.

The apprentice stood and waited breathlessly, trying not to make a sound. He didn't want to miss one note that should make its way out of this miraculous creation. Silence filled the workshop, and the Master Craftsman waited patiently and joyfully, for the best was yet to come. He looked into the questioning eyes of His apprentice and whispered, "At the beginning I gave this music box a song. Now it is making My song its own so it can give it back to Me."

Finally, a note—one strong, true note—rang out from deep within the heart of the music box. That one note echoed from the walls of the workshop, sounding over and over again, taking on a quality of tone so beautiful that tears filled the eyes of the apprentice. Suddenly the angry, violent music lashed out to fill the room again. The apprentice was alarmed, but the Master put His hand on his shoulder and waited. In the middle of the angry song a beautiful note rang out again. The angry music faltered for a moment; the true single note sounded again. Then the angry music began to decrease and dissipate as the strong, beautiful note of the mended music box sang out louder and more beautifully every time it played. Finally the true melody overpowered the angry music, banishing it from the heart of the music box forever.

And then the miracle happened. The single clear, beautiful note became two notes, then three, then four, and then multiplied into a symphony of praise to the Master Craftsman. The plain, simple song given to the little music box at its beginning had been transformed into a composition that could not be compared to anything anyone had ever heard before. The apprentice laughed joyfully, tears flowing down his cheeks, and all he could do was praise the Master Craftsman. When the symphony of praise finally ended and the Creator closed the lid, the apprentice gasped at the sight of the newly repaired music box. The broken places had been mended in such a way that the scars formed an intricate tapestry design of exceptional beauty. The once-plain, simple little trinket was now a true work of art—a masterpiece.

One day soon thereafter a family came into the workshop to ask about the lovely music box on display in the front window. The Master Craftsman tenderly picked it up and lifted the lid. A symphony emerged from deep within the heart of the small piece of art, a symphony of praise to its Creator. So impressed was the family with its beauty that they begged the Creator to sell it to them, but He told them that it was not for sale. They pleaded with Him, but He refused. Finally they asked Him to name His price, and whatever it was, they would pay it so that they could possess this tiny masterpiece. But the Craftsman said sadly, "I gave it to you once—as a gift. But you abused it and rejected it and broke its heart. Now it belongs to Me. There can be no price set on a gift." And with that, He closed the lid and gently placed the music box back where it belonged.

The family could not believe what they'd just seen and heard. This wonderful masterpiece was their own plain little music box? The last time they'd seen it, it lay in pieces in a pile of rubbish. Suddenly they realized what kind of treasure they'd once possessed, and they turned and walked sadly from the shop, mourning their great loss.

Now the music box sits in the front window of the Creator's workshop, a vivid testimony of the heart-mending power of the Master Craftsman.

~ ~ ~

Nicole Petersen is a pseudonym.

God Loves Ewe

Heide Ford

I sometimes wonder how God puts up with us.

Face it. How often has God done something incredible in your life or answered a prayer in an unbelievable way, but the next day you're faithlessly knotted up with worry? I can remember thinking that I'd never forget God's awesomeness in plucking an unknown nurse with latent writing and editing gifts and placing her at the Review and Herald to help birth *Women of Spirit* magazine. I don't want to tell you how many times since then that I've worried, doubted, or wondered what on earth God was up to in my life.

No sheepish surprises

Good thing God isn't surprised by our behavior. What reassures me about this is that God compares us to sheep. Now, little lambs may be cute, but it's not really flattering to be compared to sheep. You see, sheep are dumb. They're timid, defenseless, and easily influenced. They blindly follow any spooked sheep. In fact, a jackrabbit can frighten one and cause mass hysteria. They also maintain a butting order, tend to get into ruts, and won't lie down to rest until everyone is calm and happy. It's a wonder they get any rest at all!

But the great thing about being compared to sheep is that God says He's our shepherd. He claims us! And He takes His job very seriously. Good shepherds watch over their sheep 24/7/365. Constantly on guard for danger, they provide rich pasture grazing, go ahead of the flock to dig out poisonous weeds, apply soothing oil to bug-pestered hide, give personal attention to each one, and will do everything possible to rescue a sheep in trouble.

I'm glad the Lord is *my* shepherd—I need that kind of caring.

Cast down

A good shepherd is especially attentive when a sheep is cast down. A "cast down" sheep is flat on its back with its feet flailing in the air. Ever felt that way? I surely have. It seems that sheep can get cast down on a rather frequent basis (hmm, more similarities). Thankfully good shepherds constantly scan over the woolly heads of their flock for any sign of flailing legs.

When shepherds find a cast down sheep they talk gently to it as they begin rolling it onto its side and massaging its legs, which have lost circulation. Caressing the face and talking soothingly to the frightened and worn animal, the shepherd straddles the sheep, lifting it to its feet and holding it steady. Wobble, wobble, fall is the routine—numerous times even, but each time the shepherd lifts the sheep back up and steadies it. Staying with the sheep until strength returns to its legs, the shepherd then leads it gently home.

What a picture of what God does for you and me!

Are you cast down? Are you frightened or worn? Jesus, your good shepherd, is right by your side. In your exasperated condition you many not sense Him, but listen closely—He's talking soothingly to you. He's there to lift you up, to steady you, to restore your soul.

"The Lord is my shepherd; I have everything I need. . . . Even when I walk through the dark valley . . . you are close beside me. . . . My cup overflows with blessings" (Ps. 23:1-5, NLT).*

---

*Scripture quotations marked NLT are taken from the *Holy Bible*, New Living Translation, copyright © 1996. Used by permission of Tyndale House Publishers, Inc., Wheaton, Illinois 60189. All rights reserved.

~ ~ ~

Heide Ford, associate editor of *Women of Spirit*, loves reading, spring flowers, and whale watching. She and her husband live in Maryland.

I Need You

Faith Ann Laughlin

I need you, Mommy."

My almost-3-year-old stretches up his arms, begging to be carried. Somewhere he has come up with this all-purpose phrase. "I need you" means: I'm tired. I'm lonely. I want to sleep. I'm hungry and want to watch you make supper. I don't want you to leave me.

I can't feel you

Recently the academy where I work held a student-versus-staff softball game on Saturday night. The game started late after sundown. By 8:30 on most nights my boy has sawn enough logs for a small tree house. Yet here we sat on the cold bleachers, K.J. wrapped in a fuzzy blanket, me with my unused ball glove between my feet. His plaintive insistent cries had pulled me from the game before it even started. I held him close. Time will fly, and one day I may be the one crying "I need you, son." He wriggled on my lap. He squirmed this way and that. I tightened the blanket against the cold night air.

"What's wrong, son?" I asked.

"I can't *feel* you."

Then I remembered. Since I'd weaned him more than six months ago he has fallen into the habit of putting his hand on my neck when I hold him or rock him. Wrapped in the tight bundle of blankets he could not reach out to feel me.

I settled him back on my lap, still swaddled in the blanket but just loose enough for one little hand to pat Mommy's neck. He drifted contentedly off into a sound sleep.

Needing God's touch

How often do we reach out to our heavenly Father?

"I need You, Lord." He picks us up and holds us tightly. As we squirm and wiggle in His loving embrace, we cry out, "Father, I can't feel You."

We know He is there. We know He loves us immensely and eternally, but we can't feel Him.

Recently our family moved from one coast to the other. Close friends have become long-distance friends. Long-distance family has become "just an hour down the road" family. We have traded one good for another. Yet at times we deeply miss the fellowship with our friends.

God slipped into my thoughts one afternoon as I sat longing for the times when I prayed together with my closest friend. Praying with her brought a feeling of God's presence.

You don't need to wait for someone else before praying. Pray when you feel the need. I am still here.

"OK, Lord. Here I am. I have been testing students and grading papers and working furiously for days. I am worn out. I need to know that someone loves me and believes in me."

ILY from God

I love you, My daughter. Have you seen the way that daddies look at their little girls? Have you seen the love in Kenny's eyes as he looks at Katie Ann? Do you remember the way Michael used to look at Jillian? It would send you running from the room in pain from being a fatherless child.

"Yes, I remember. It doesn't hurt as it once did."

I love you in that way. Only hundreds and thousands of times more than what you see in their eyes. I love you, My child. I believe in you.

"Wow." I said, blinking back the tears. "I'd forgotten. Thank You for that reminder."

You're welcome.

Use us to touch

Lord, help us today to see a weary child who needs to feel Your presence. Use us to touch each other, so that we all might feel Your arms of love around us.

Remind us that You walk with us, even when we can't feel You. In the name of Jesus, Amen.

~ ~ ~

Faith Ann Laughlin, a reading specialist, currently teaches Spanish to kindergarten and first-grade kids in the public school system. She and her husband, Ken, have a daughter and son.

Did You Say Something?

Kim Peckham

Have you ever been lending an ear to a friend—nodding your head with interest and maintaining sincere eye contact—and realized that you were, in fact, not listening? It's as if your brain takes a 20-second vacation to the Bahamas and makes it back to the office just in time to hear the other person say, ". . . so be sure to avoid eating any of that until they trace the killer bacteria."

This happens to me quite often. It happens even while I am listening to my wife—which, let me tell you, does nothing to enhance the sweet bonds of marriage.

Maybe it's a side effect of age, like rheumatism and an affection for Cracker Barrel restaurants. Or maybe it's because there's a lot of talking in the world, and it's hard to take it all in.

For instance, consider those automated phone-answering systems. The voice might be the most pleasant in the world, but the subject matter lacks drama. So after the first 60 seconds of hearing which buttons to push, my mind has run off to join the circus.

And what about those safety instructions they give you on airplanes, describing which end of the metal buckle should be firmly grasped? If you can listen all the way through that spiel with rapt attention, your Ritalin dosage is too high.

Sermons provide another way to test a person's attentiveness. I take great pleasure in reminding my friend Larry about the time I saw him doze off during a sermon on the subject of—get this—the evils of sloth.

I think God in His mercy protects pastors from knowing how far the minds of the congregation wander during sermons. While the pastor is preaching sanctification, people in the pews might be pondering subjects of less than eternal significance, such as *Who's supposed to be sharpening the pencils by the tithe envelopes?*

I know it would put a lot of pressure on clergy, but what if we could measure the attentiveness of the congregation in the same way that TV programs measure their audience? At the end of the service the pastor would get a report of the percentage of people who tuned in: sermon—71 percent; children's story—84 percent; potluck announcement—99 percent.

If I may say so, the whole problem with lecturing is that it's so one-sided. In any other verbal encounter that lasts for more than five minutes, most of us expect an opportunity to mention our back pain and the accomplishments of at least two or three grandchildren. If there's going to be talking, we like to take turns.

Person 1: "I've got a bit of a headache."

Person 2: "Yeah, well, I've got this mole that looks a little like the state of Kentucky."

Person 1: "Oh, really? Well, in the summer of '87, I canned about 20 quarts of peaches."

Person 2: "That reminds me—do you know that little Buster can play 'Indian Reservation' on the piano?"

Person 1: " Great! Say, does this sweater make me look fat?"

Apparently, even if you have give-and-take in a conversation, it doesn't mean anyone is listening. And listening is a good thing. We all know that. We expect God to listen to our prayers all the time, and we take for granted that His attention doesn't wander.

But we will have a richer relationship with Him if we add Bible study to our prayer life. In that way we're listening to what God has to say—even if our attention does wander from time to time.

~ ~ ~

Kim Peckham is the director of advertising for the Review and Herald Publishing Association. He has been a columnist for *Women of Spirit* since its first issue. He says that he and his wife live in one of the Virginia states. He isn't sure which. He's not been paying attention.

More Than a Daughter

Katie Tonn-Oliver

I really love where we live," Ge-Ge says, looking out from their hilltop at the tree-covered mountains. She loves the privacy. No curious eyes look into their windows.

Ge-Ge grew up in a "glass house." As the daughter of world-famous SDA radio evangelist of the Voice of Prophecy, H.M.S. Richards, Sr., people often drove slowly by their home for a firsthand look at how they lived. Many weren't content just to drive by, but would stop, come up to the house, and peer into the windows.

No wonder Ge-Ge guards her privacy now, keeping close to her heart the things most precious to her. The knowledge that her story can encourage others enables her to share with people today.

Somebody's daughter

H.M.S. Richards, Sr., was an ordinary man who became extraordinary because of his relationship with God. He had the gift to make biblical stories and precepts come alive for those who heard him speak.

"I was 12 years old, skinny, gawky, flat-chested, with big feet," Ge-Ge says with a smile, "when my dad gave me an incredible blessing. We were at a large meeting, and it was time for Dad to go on to another appointment. As usual, he was always surrounded by people, and Mom sent me to tell him it was time to go. I remember going shyly to that group of men and slipping up behind Dad to give his coat a tug. He turned and pulled me right up under his arm and said, 'Gentlemen, I want you to meet Virginia Dale Elizabeth Richards, my daughter. She is the light of my life.'

"It took me many years to realize the incredible gift my father gave me with those words. The gift of total acceptance, of a father's pride in his adolescent daughter, and of his unbounded love."

It was a wonderful legacy to be the daughter of H.M.S. Richards, Sr., but it was often a burden to be the child of a famous and beloved man. It was easy for people to expect—or demand—that his children should be one way or another. Yet her parents did their best to keep such pressure off their children.

"My mother was a great believer in allowing her youngsters the greatest freedom possible. For example, in the front room you could hear the little band my brother pulled together playing jazzy tunes. If we wanted to go ice skating, Mother went with us. If we wanted to go to the movies—provided the film had redemptive value—Mother went with us. I was allowed to play any music I wanted in my own room, as long as the door was closed and the volume was low. I could wear shorts, even rolling them up to make them shorter, in our house and backyard. Things like this helped keep my life normal.

"On the important things, of course, Mother wouldn't budge an inch. Reverence for the Sabbath, concern for the welfare and feelings of others, respect for our elders, honesty, and more. At the core of Mother's parenting was the concept that her children—their personhood and freedom—were more important than what other people thought. She and Dad respected us first, so it was easy for us to respect them!

"By their lives and attitude they gave us a model of how God treats us all, loving us first so we can respond to Him."

It's no wonder that Ge-Ge's relationship with God makes her extraordinary too. At age 13 she was baptized by her father, along with her best friend. She's never regretted her decision, but it was 30 years later, when she joined a five-year program of disciplined Bible study, that she "fell in love with Jesus."

Somebody's love

Ge-Ge was attracted to Walt Cason because, as she jokes, "he was tall enough that I could wear really high heels that made my ankles look small. Wearing the heels also gave me an excuse to cling to his arm as we walked. We liked that!" They had four children, and Ge-Ge followed in her mother's footsteps as a work widow. In the first years of their marriage Walt was overseas in the Army during World War II. Then he was in medical school, followed by private practice. His career often kept him away from home. Like her mother, Ge-Ge almost single-handedly raised her children. Like her mother, Ge-Ge is a strong, spunky, independent woman.

Though she no longer wears high, high heels, she still clings to Walt's arm. Romance, and their deep love for each another, remain a big part of their lives.

Ge-Ge has done many things other women just dream about—piloting a plane, working for 10 years at KCDS gospel radio, and going to modeling school. She was in her early 40s and feeling rather dowdy, so she decided to do something about it. "The six-month course taught me how to stand and walk with grace," she says, "and the makeup class was called 'Make Down.' I learned to put on the minimal amount of cosmetics for a great look." She'd recommend such a course to anyone.

Somebody's mother

Decades ago four young children filled their home with squeals and laughter. Years later, four young adults were ready to meet the world. Then, without warning, there were only three.

On June 1, 1972, Elizabeth Rae, age 19, died in an auto accident. Two weeks after her death the county installed a traffic signal that residents had been requesting for several years.

"Her death almost broke my heart, of course. Elizabeth Rae, my ray of sunlight. Afterward I told myself, *I can make it for five years without her, and then Jesus will come.* But the five years passed, so I thought, *I guess I could live through another five years.* But when 10 years had passed, it was hard to say to myself, *I stuck it out for 10 years; I suppose I can go for another 10.* Now it's been more than 20 without my 'sunshine.' I'll always miss her."

Their second child was an attorney in a law firm when she was diagnosed with Hodgkin's disease. On several occasions Ge-Ge drove to her town to take her to the hospital for chemotherapy and radiation treatments. Eventually the Hodgkin's went into remission, and her prognosis is good. "But I feared that we'd lose her, too," Ge-Ge admits.

Their lastborn is a professional woman. She writes, paints, is a flutist and occasionally writes book reviews.

Then there is Marshall, their creative, imaginative firstborn. Their only son, who died of complications from the AIDS virus in September 1995.

After graduating from college, Marshall more or less disappeared from their lives. Only a few times during the long, long years of estrangement did his family even have an address where they could reach him. Neither Ge-Ge nor Walt understood what was wrong, what had driven him away. They worried about him and yearned over him and time and again committed him to God's care, while Ge-Ge claimed the promise of Proverbs 11:21: "The seed of the righteous shall be delivered."

While he was abroad, Marshall wrote his parents to tell them he was a homosexual. His mother wrote back: "We love you. That will never change, no matter what."

"It's easy to try to relive the past," Ge-Ge says. *"If only we had understood Marshall's struggles!"*

Ge-Ge took a leave of absence from her volunteer job at KCDS so she could be with Marshall, who now required full-time care. Sometimes she just dropped by to watch him sleep. "I longed to pick him up in my arms and take away all the hurt he felt all his life," she'll tell you. "I am his mother!"

Minnesota 1992 watershed

"I went to speak at a Minnesota women's retreat with instructions from God that I must tell about Marshall, that he was a PWA, a person with AIDS. But I just couldn't. Friday night I spoke about the idealism I had as a young mother and about my broken dreams, but I couldn't talk about Marshall being gay or tell them that he had AIDS."

Agatha Richardson and her friend Wilma Lewis, listening to Ge-Ge speak, looked at her face and then at her photograph printed in their program. It didn't look like the same person. Ge-Ge the speaker had no life to her, no joy.

"I was tired and worn and burdened," Ge-Ge later told a friend. "When I got up to speak, nothing even made sense to me. Agatha and Wilma knew, and came to my room to pray with me. They asked me about what was burdening me, and I told them about Marshall. They prayed for nearly two hours, asking God to fill me with His Holy Spirit and open Marshall's heart to love. I've never experienced something to this deep degree in prayer. I felt the power of the Holy Spirit, who gave me words to speak. I could talk about Marshall, and I felt confident that God's promise would come true: my son would be delivered."

When Ge-Ge told the two women of Marshall's anger, Wilma said, "Marshall's anger is a test for all of us, to see if we'll respond in love or not. When you know in whom you believe, you look beyond the anger and see Jesus. You find Him in an angry face longing for love. We're all so deeply scarred by sin. We need to hear—no matter what—how much God loves us."

And now, three years after the Minnesota retreat, Marshall is dead. In his last days of life, through the power of intercessory prayer, he made peace with his family. He forgave those who had hurt him beyond understanding.

Did the promise Ge-Ge had claimed for so many years come true? Before his death many miracles occurred in Marshall's life, and she had reason to believe the promise had been fulfilled. But . . . "Please," a mother's heart cried out to God. "Can I *know* the promise is true?"

In a conversation with his father just a few days before his death, Marshall was finally able to say, "I want heaven. I want to see you there." And he arranged to meet his mother and father at the tree of life.

Despite her deep friendship with God, despite the support and friendship of others, Ge-Ge often has felt desperately lonely. During the early years of Marshall's illness she longed for someone at her church to put an arm around her, to whisper, "I'm so sorry your son is sick. I'm praying for you." She had lived in a "glass house" for so long, and had been open about Marshall's illness and its cause, that she thought the "rumor mill would have ground out the bad news." So when few comforted her, she thought they were rejecting her. During the last months of Marshall's life, though, as people became aware of her burdens, many hugs and phone calls sustained her.

But people don't know what to say when a mother's gay son has AIDS, so too often they stay away. And because she is the daughter of H.M.S. Richards, Sr., people still tend to think she has all the answers. That she doesn't have questions of her own.

"We must remember our spiritual leaders—our teachers and pastors, or women's ministry directors—are people of like passions, ones who need to know we're praying for them. We shouldn't ascribe to them more power than we have ourselves. We are all equally empowered by God to be and become His children."

Last words from Ge-Ge

"Sometimes part of me yearns to be a child again. Sometimes I just want to crawl into my daddy's lap and cry my heart out. So I get as close to the lap of God as I can, and cry there.

"In our spiritual lives it's important to get to the basics. Jesus loves *me! ME!* Warts and all! I also think women need to know as much about themselves as possible, because it is through your *self* that Jesus wants to live in you. Each of us is different, and beautiful from the inside out. And being in a relationship with Jesus makes us the most beautiful we can be.

"These are the words I want those who know me to hold close to their hearts—just as Jesus loves me, Jesus loves YOU.

"Just as you are."

~ ~ ~

Katie Tonn-Oliver is a freelance, creative, and commercial writer living in Paradise, California. She and Virginia Cason have been dear friends for many years.

Putting the Bears to Bed

Leigh Anderson

"Daddy, would you tuck in the bears?"

Lisa and her dad shared this nighttime ritual for 24 years. Then, on a perfect June evening, it all changed. Arm-in-arm father and daughter walked down the flower-strewn church aisle. A tear glistened on her cheek.

The wedding and reception over, they embraced one last time, and Lisa made the same childhood request. Then the limousine disappeared down the road.

~ ~ ~

We'd been discussing the high cost of tires with Chris, and the possible advantage of group buying, so when he called and asked if Dennis and I would both be home that evening, I assumed he wanted to follow up on the tire conversation. Chris was Lisa's boyfriend. They'd met 10 years earlier, had been each other's first love, then had gone their separate ways. After completing college at opposite ends of the country, they were reunited when Chris came to town to begin medical school. We were chatting comfortably that evening when Chris casually said, "I would like to ask Lisa to marry me. Would that be OK with you?"

Wow! Quite a switch from talking tires.

Months have passed since Lisa and Chris's wedding. Emotions, some mysterious and unfamiliar, still find their way into my consciousness. I really wasn't prepared for my new role and relationship. I was unsure how to transition from involved parent to parent emeritus. No one warned me about the grief and sense of loss that follows a wedding. What do you say to friends when they knowingly smile and ask about the "joys" of a quiet, child-free house? No, I am not depressed, and I don't want to be 35 again. I just wish someone had told me how it was going to be when my only daughter married.

I'd always thought that "getting married" was a specific event. Now I know that it is a collection of complex changes experienced over a period of time. The marriage of a child is different from any other parenting milestone. It's not time-specific, like giving birth or high school graduation.

During the six months that Lisa and Chris were engaged, we slowly became new people: mother-in-law, father-in-law, sister-in-law, brother-in-law, husband, wife. Each day during their engagement Lisa and Chris were "getting married." This was evident as they started making more and more decisions together. Simple tasks like purchasing the bed for their new home, balancing their joint checking account, and deciding whether Ben and Jerry or Lady Lee would occupy their freezer—all were a part of this process.

Many people contributed toward their "getting married." Our house painter refinished several pieces of well-used furniture for them—without charge; the local film processing lab surprised them with an 8-x-10 copy of their engagement photo; the retired band conductor hired to arrange the music for the bridal processional declined payment. Daily best wishes, many accompanied by generous gifts, nudged the passage onward.

We learned that heartstoppers—unplanned events—are common during the "getting married" months. With deliberate good humor we awaited our share. In April a friend's freezer went on the fritz. Its entire contents was ruined, including all of the baked goods intended for Lisa's shower. But friends rallied around, baked up a storm, and provided more than enough fresh goodies. Two weeks before the wedding a key musician canceled. We endured a momentary panic, then found a wonderful replacement.

For the older generation, the young lovers' "getting married" months were a poignant time of remembering. Unmarried brothers and sisters and cousins spent the time dreaming, planning, and moving closer to making their own marriage commitments.

Most often Lisa and Chris were cheerful, enjoying this in-between time. But sometimes, when wedding plans were especially demanding, they seemed a bit overwhelmed and impatient with the whole experience.

The wedding weekend, three celebration-filled days, provided the finishing touches to "getting married." Surrounded by a hubbub of family and friends we enjoyed leisurely meals, worship, and laughter. Then on Sunday afternoon, as the shadows began to lengthen, a seriousness came over each one of us as we gathered in the church. In soft yet confident tones Lisa and Chris promised to love and hold each other dear . . . forever. Imperceptibly they transitioned from "getting married" to being married, a profound change in the way they would think ever after.

Dennis and I returned to the church around midnight. We were weary, yet sleep eluded us. Silently, hand in hand, we sat in the front pew, finding comfort in the lingering fragrance of gardenias and roses. Memories of Lisa's baby dedication, baptism, and academy graduation—all held in that same sanctuary—came to mind. Someone had left a wedding program. We picked it up and relived the events of the day. We found comfort in the knowledge that Jesus chose a wedding weekend over any other occasion to begin His public ministry.

The newlyweds live a few blocks from us. We try very hard not to intrude into their lives. When they choose to come over it is like rain to a dry land. The other evening Lisa came by to pick up some more of her things, and Dennis helped her carry the boxes down to her car. As they were leaving her room he told her, "Don't forget the bears."

She seemed puzzled. "Why can't they stay?"

A long pause. "Because the bears need to be tucked in every night," Dennis said slowly. "Without you to remind me, I may forget."

~ ~ ~

Leigh Anderson, an outpatient surgery center administrator, lives with her husband, Dennis, in southern California. They have two adult children and are active in short-term mission trips. Leigh enjoys entertaining university students.

Tornado Touchdown

Sally Pierson Dillon

Speeding down the freeway, I scowled at the black clouds hovering overhead. I'd done an extra load of laundry instead of listening to a weather report, so this was a surprise. Of course, when news and weather conflicted with *Sesame Street,* it was never much of a contest. I just hoped the rain wouldn't start until the car was parked and I was safely in the hospital to start my evening shift.

As I pulled up the expressway ramp toward the tollbooth, my vision suddenly blanked out. I blinked and stared at the windshield, but there was nothing there. I had a terrible feeling of disequilibrium, and a sensation of utter silence that seemed to last forever. Then my tires hit the pavement with a loud smack. Feeling totally disoriented, I looked around. My car was still on the ramp, but facing the wrong way. The car that had been behind me now was in front of me. It slowly backed down the ramp, and I followed it and pulled back onto the Stevenson Expressway. What was wrong with me? How did I get myself backwards on the steep-sided ramp? There was no way I could have turned around even if I'd done the tightest donut. I was taking medication for a seizure disorder, but this was unlike anything I'd experienced before. Could it have been a seizure?

Work didn't seem important now. I carefully drove back to my mother-in-law's house to pick up Donnie. From there I called in sick for my afternoon shift, and slowly drove home. I spent the rest of the afternoon on the couch, trying to figure out what had happened.

When Bruce got home, I tried to explain the puzzling events to him. As we talked, Donnie turned on the TV. The local news was in progress. "The tornado touched down right there on the on ramp," a tollway attendant was explaining. "It picked up a little red Chevette and carried it way up into the air, then plunked it back down right on the ramp but facing the wrong way. The woman driving it didn't bat an eyelid. She just drove slowly back down the ramp—the wrong way—and got back on the expressway as though she did this every day!"

Donnie opened the front door and stared out at my little red Chevette in the driveway. "Mama, was that you?" he asked as Bruce and I, riveted by the TV account, sank to our knees.

"Yes," I finally whispered. "That was me."

Later that night I thought about how we'd prayed that morning. As we always did, we asked God to protect Bruce as he drove to and from work; and we asked for His care over Donnie and me as we spent the day together, that He would cup us in the hollow of His big strong hands and keep us safe. Even now I can't think about that day without picturing His big hands cupped around me, Chevette and all.

How literally He takes our prayers! How tenderly He cares for us, no matter what the situation. Surely I can trust the God who gently cradled me through the vortex of a tornado to guide me through whatever traumas today might bring.

~ ~ ~

Sally Pierson Dillon, a prolific author and mother of two adult sons, does her best to keep all four wheels on the ground. She and her husband live in New Market, Virginia.

When I Looked at the Cross

Karen Nicola

I had never been at the foot of a literal cross before. I wondered if I'd ever been there in my mind and heart. At the foot of the cross, my heart experienced nearly every emotion possible. It happened one morning at a beautiful Christian retreat center in the Santa Cruz mountains. It had been a while since I'd enjoyed solitude with my God, and I cherished every moment of our quiet intimacy.

It was announced that a group hike to the cross on the retreat property would leave early Friday morning. The group would watch the sunrise. The cross sounded like a special place to enjoy the presence of my Lord, but knowing it had the potential of reaching deep into my soul, I wasn't comfortable going in a large group.

I thought about going alone, but since I was new to the retreat grounds, I wanted someone to go with me. So I asked my new friend, Maggie, if she would join me. We made plans to go on Thursday morning.

Setting out early while the sky was still gray-blue, Maggie and I had two immediate challenges. First, the entire hike was uphill, and second, neither of us had been there before. We relied on our memory of directions others had given. The road twisted and turned as it climbed the hill. We'd been walking nearly 30 minutes when the pavement ended and a path led off through the woods. We were surprised not to see any signs indicating the way.

"I remember hearing that the cross wasn't that impressive a site anyway," Maggie puffed as we began the dirt path.

"Let's go a little farther and see for ourselves," I replied.

The path seemed to parallel the mountain. We thought for sure that we'd be able to spot the cross by now, but the trees and shrubs continued to block our view of the top of the hill. We began to doubt that we'd ever find it. Maybe we took the wrong road at the beginning. There were two roads to choose from. Maybe we'd missed a major direction sign while we were talking. We were tiring. The incline was taking its toll. Maybe we ought to chalk up the morning as a good workout and go back.

Maggie was just about to suggest that we turn back when we saw the sun rising over a clearing toward the top of the hill. There it was—the cross! As we continued the last part of our hike, I pondered Jesus' weakness (or should I say strength?) as He made that walk so long ago. Our chests heaved trying to fill our lungs with air needed for the climb. When we finally reached the cross, we collapsed at its base. Is this what it means when God's Word says, "Let us labor therefore to enter in to that rest" (Heb. 4:11, KJV)? Suddenly, resting in Jesus took on new meaning.

Except for our heavy breathing, there was no sound as we leaned back against the cross, watching the rising sun. We sat in silence for a long while. Jesus' sacrifice began to take on a reality I had never known. I kept having an irresistible urge to turn and look up to the top of the cross, but I pushed the thought away, for I knew it would break my heart. I'm so afraid of pain. Dare I look into my Saviour's face? What would His eyes say should they meet mine?

Maggie and I talked a bit about the reality of Christ in our lives. She'd been a Christian only a short time, while I had had many years of precious moments with my Lord. But somehow as we sat there together, we sensed an equality of both time and experience.

That morning at the cross will remain forever in my memory. I learned of my need of companionship on my journey toward the cross. Without each other, neither Maggie nor I would have reached it. The fellowship kept us encouraged and seeking. Although I love my solitude with God, I am thankful for fellow travelers who keep hope alive when I doubt.

We decided it would be special to pray together before going back. As we turned to kneel facing the cross, I lifted my eyes to the place where Jesus' face would have been. For a second—that I pray will last a lifetime—I looked into His face. His look penetrated my being, and my heart was broken. I saw compassion and understanding in His eyes. I saw His eyes full of forgiveness and acceptance. I saw eyes filled with hope and renewal.

I saw the eyes of God, and suddenly I saw my own in vivid contrast. My eyes were filled with condemnation, censure, partiality, criticism, and complaint. It took only a second's glance to break my heart, to show me my barrenness and apply the desperately needed eye salve so I could see, in that moment, as God sees.

I want to look daily into Jesus' face as He hung, dying for me on the cross, that by beholding I may be changed.

~ ~ ~

Karen Nicola, a speaker and author of several books, was pursuing a master's in elementary education when she wrote this article. She loves to decorate, spin wool, and play her recorder. She and her husband have two children.

Happy Heart Day

Jewell Johnson

The home-baked cupcakes sprinkled with candy hearts were ready to go. I was looking forward to Valentine's Day *and* our girls' Bible club meeting. As the sponsor, I'd decorated cupcakes and planned a Valentine craft. The girls would trade handmade valentines, too.

But I wanted more. Preteen girls can be very critical, so I saw this as a time to help them see the good in each other. I decided to have them trade spoken valentines—words of appreciation from their hearts.

But when I got to class I had second thoughts. While the regular girls chatted and laughed together, a new girl sat hunched at the end of the table. Her name was Julie.

Should I scrap my valentine idea? What positive thing could Julie say to girls she doesn't know? And what might they say to her?

I had further doubts when I noticed Brandy. Three months earlier a dog had attacked her, tearing her left cheek and leaving a large, jagged, red scar on her flawless skin. The wound had healed, but the scar ate at Brandy's confidence, and she often hid it with her hand. Also, she'd started turning sideways when speaking to people. Should I risk someone making a thoughtless remark about her scar?

In spite of my doubts, I decided to go ahead.

"Valentine's Day is a time to show love and appreciation for our friends," I told the girls. "I want you to think of something you appreciate about the girl next to you and tell her. It will be a spoken valentine. I'll begin."

I turned to Brenda. "I appreciate your faithful attendance in girls' club, Brenda. You work to memorize the Bible verses, and you have a great attitude."

5

Brenda thought a moment, then looked at the girl next to her. "You are real friendly and have a nice smile."

Without hesitation Justine turned to Julie, the new girl. "You seem like a nice person, someone I'd like to have for my friend."

Now it was Julie's turn. What would she say to Brandy, a girl she hadn't met until today?

Julie turned to Brandy. Her shyness lifted, and with a glowing smile Julie said, "You're so pretty!"

"Oh!" Brandy gasped. Her hand raised to cover her cheek, then dropped to her side. Her eyes shone. She straightened in her chair. Smiling, she turned to give the girl beside her a valentine.

Did Julie see Brandy's scar? Of course. But God allowed her to see more. Her valentine assured Brandy that true friends see beyond scars and flaws. For when you see with your heart, you see the heart.

~ ~ ~

Jewell Johnson writes from Fountain Hills, Arizona. A retired R.N., she enjoys walking and quilting.

My Friend Shari

Judye Beth Estes

I could say that Shari smoked like a chimney, cussed like a sailor, and drank like a fish, but that's not entirely true—she drank ice water. She was also my best and dearest friend for 20 years.

We were like the odd couple. She was messy; I was neat. She was brave; I was chicken. She was outgoing; I was shy.

She was articulate. She'd say, "He is so volatile." I'd say, "He sure gets mad easily."

She'd say, "He has a voracious appetite." I'd say, "He sure eats a lot."

She was worldly-wise; I was naive. And our unlikely alliance came about like this.

A new pizza parlor provided a band playing Texas country along with their pizza, and I, working but living with my parents, started going there. Every time we went, we saw Shari. She sat with the "in crowd," socializing with Jerry, the band leader.

For a year or more I saw her from across the room, sitting with her (no-good) husband* and their two kids. Then the band moved across town to Shakey's pizza, and we followed. Between music, Jerry talked with the customers. My mother was always friendly and funny. My dad sat quietly, dignified in his dress shirt and tie. Jerry called him "the senator." "Hello, Senator," he'd call across the room, and people would whisper, "Look, there's a senator!"

Going it alone

Then my mother died suddenly, and my dad began to spend months in Tennessee with my sister. I trekked across town to Shakey's alone. I'd bring a book and read between music sets, and Jerry would stop by and say, "You really should get to know Shari. You'd like her." But no, not me. I didn't have the nerve to cross the room and talk to her.

Then one night she got up and strode to my table. She pulled herself up to her almost-five-feet and said haughtily, "You can come sit with us if you want."

How could I refuse such a *cordial* invitation? I picked up my book and joined the "in crowd."

We laughed about it later, her icy invitation. "Why were you so haughty?" I'd ask her, and she'd say, "You were such a prissy little Goody Two-shoes, and Jerry bragged on you all the time. He thought you were so perfect."

"Me? He thought *you* were so perfect."

Shari's gifts to me

Shari gave me her phone number that first night, should I want to call. I wanted to, all right, but she had all these friends; she didn't need me. Days passed. I held the scrap of paper, read it, stared at it—and at last got up my nerve. She was tickled I'd called, and we began doing things together. Now *I* sat with the in crowd at Shakey's, and on Saturday nights after it closed down we might go out to breakfast with Jerry. Or we'd go shopping at an all-night store—her kids coming too—then sit on her patio till the sun came up, just talking. If anyone knew the secrets of my soul, Shari did, and she kept them very well.

She gave me the gift of laughter. I'm not a "belly laugher." If something's really funny to me, I smile. But with Shari, I laughed a lot. Things were hilarious when we were together. One Sunday afternoon we went to a restaurant and found it almost empty. It was so quiet that our whispering echoed as if we were shouting. "Maybe this isn't a restaurant at all," Shari leaned over and murmured. "Maybe it's a front for a funeral parlor."

I began to laugh, and then to snort, and the next thing I knew I saw an insect floating in my soup. "Shari! There's a spider in my soup," I gasped.

She leaned over to look. "Or it's your false eyelashes."

Shari gave me the gift of loyalty. When changes at work made me quit my job, she stood up for me. She went with me to help me clean out my office, and even though I felt like crying, with Shari I could hold up my head—and laugh.

Shari modeled Christian hospitality to me. Anyone who needed a place to stay was welcome at her house—for weeks or months. It wasn't unusual to have a down-and-outer bunking in a spare room. She wasn't judgmental. She just gave them a place to sort out their lives and get on their feet again.

Then Shari got a new job and met a man named Bob. They became friends, then good friends. They began to date, and eventually Bob wanted to marry.

Planning our leisure years

I moved to Maryland. We kept in touch, Shari and I. When I went back to Texas two summers later we celebrated Christmas. One time she flew up to see me. We always planned that in our old age I'd move back to Texas and we'd spend our sunset years in leisure together.

Just four years ago I picked up the ringing telephone to hear a man's voice. "Judye, has anyone from here called you yet?" it asked. It was Shari's son.

"It's bad news," he said. "Mother died this morning."

No!

Not Shari. Not my best and dearest friend, who gave me self-confidence and laughter. Not the girlfriend who cleaned up her mouth because of me and who taught me to look beyond outward appearances and into one's soul.

If I have learned one thing it is that if we are openhearted God can bring friendships into our lives that will enrich us beyond imagining. That's what He did—for both Shari and me—when He nudged her to walk across the room and, nose in the air, ask if I wanted to come sit at her table.

---

*He always ran around on her, and eventually they separated. He acquired a "new wife" while he still had an "old wife," and finally he and Shari divorced.

~ ~ ~

Judye Beth Estes, an avid Dallas Cowboy fan, is senior list specialist for periodical subscriptions at the Review and Herald. She's a whiz-bang Scrabble player and enjoys battling it out with her nephew, Tompaul.

A Vessel for the Lord

Blanche Yates

"Can I not do with you as this potter?" says the Lord. "Look, as the clay is in the potter's hand, so are you in My hand" (Jer. 18:6, NKJV).*
I once thought that as a vessel for my Lord to use I was a crystal vase or golden bowl, created for special use—with unique gifts given by Him. I felt that I only needed some cleaning and polishing to be ready for the Master's special purpose. To be used "for such a time as this."

But as time has passed and the Lord has cleaned me off and shined me up, I've come to realize that no "special" or "exciting" work awaits me. For He has called me for day-to-day use. I am His washpot. His utility pail. I am serviceable, but not exciting. Necessary—but my beauty comes from my usefulness to Him and His reflected glory in my shiny sides. It is an imperfect likeness at best.

Mine will not be the lot of honor or power or might through Him, but of just living, doing my simple, humble, daily tasks to His honor and glory. My battles are not earthshaking, my victories not grand and mighty.

Uncommon tasks

It is true that at times the Master has given me some uncommon tasks. He has used me to carry some heavy responsibilities and even to put out a few fires. But I was fashioned for utility, for usefulness. I have found that I can be happy whether I'm filled with lovely flowers from the garden, or dirt. I can be happy when I'm used for carrying pure, fresh cold water, or soapy water for scrubbing.

I will never grace a beautiful table or have others gasp at my exquisite design and beauty. I'm not exhibited at banquets or displayed before spe-

50

cial games. But I do have my own special place. And they choose me first when there is a need. I am sturdy. I can take the heat. I am not marred by strong solutions or easily broken by careless hands. I am dependable and trustworthy. I help to keep the Master's house clean and shiny. I daily get to work in His service.

Although I am not exquisite or delicate, I do have beauty of design. There is poetry in my soul, and I inspire others to sing as they work. My lot is a happy one, for I enjoy what I do. I am functional and valuable. Humility becomes me. Submissiveness agrees with me. Even when I'm in storage and not in service, I am good at holding other smaller things safely.

I do admire the crystal vase with its single rosebud and the golden bowl on display. But I accept the role that the Master has given me. I will promote the health and happiness of others. I will cheerfully serve Him every day in the work He designed me for. I was not meant to be protected in a closet or displayed behind glass doors. I was created for service. "For such a time as this" is today and every day for me.

---

*Texts credited to NKJV are from The New King James Version. Copyright © 1979, 1980, 1982, Thomas Nelson, Inc., Publishers.

~ ~ ~

Blanche Yates enjoys computers, music, and writing and working with computers. She and her husband, Lee, have five children.

Would My Aneurysm Burst?

Carlene Hacker

One minute I was fine, driving along on my way to a friend's house. The next moment I saw double. I blinked, trying to focus my eyes. Blinked again. The double images remained. So I gripped the steering wheel, slowed down, and tried not to panic.

That evening I told my husband, Al, what had happened. Puzzled, we went to our trusty medical book and found that double vision (diplopia) could mean a tumor or aneurysm, the ballooning of a weakened artery. Al wrapped his arms around me, and we held each other. "Tell me again what happened," he said.

I sighed and repeated my story. "It lasted about 10 minutes," I concluded. "And my head hurt terribly."

"You've been having headaches for a while," he told me.

My head still nestled on his shoulder. "We're not getting any younger," I said. "This probably won't amount to anything."

Al continued to hold me. Fear rose in my throat. "I think I'll call the optometrist."

That night we phoned our son, Scott, an orthopedic surgical resident at the University of Washington in Seattle. Telling him what happened, I added, "The optometrist said it was probably a random incident."

"Mom," he cried, "you go to your doctor for double vision. It isn't something to fool around with."

"Scott, you're scaring me."

"Sorry, Mom, but this is important. How long did it last?"

"About 10 minutes at its worst."

"Call your doctor, Mom. See him tomorrow."

God's promise

That night I read Psalm 31:15, "My times are in your hands." The simple words were filled with God's comforting presence. Somehow I knew they would sustain me through the long winter season ahead.

My doctor called a week later, and his report was staggering. "Your MRI reveals a small aneurysm on your left ophthalmic artery. It's not large, but I want you to see a neurologist as soon as possible." Stunned, I slumped into a chair.

The earliest the neurologist could see me was one month later. By then I'd had two more episodes of diplopia. His blunt diagnosis was bone-chilling. "You have a life-threatening situation. I want to hospitalize you this afternoon." Then calling Al and a neurosurgeon into the office, he described treatment: an angiogram first, brain surgery the next day. Reeling with shock, we hurried home to call Scott.

"Look, I talked to Dr. Richard Winn, our chair of the Department of Neurological Surgery," Scott told me. "He'll see you whenever you come. Go ahead with the angiogram, but I want you to see Dr. Winn for a second opinion. He specializes in aneurysms and has done hundreds of these surgeries. Come anytime. Come tomorrow."

We were in Dr. Winn's office four days later. His calm manner and knowledge of aneurysms was assuring. We trusted him. After additional tests he recommended surgery within six months. "If you don't have it by then, because you are Scott's mom, I will worry."

With my family and friends worried about me, I found comfort surrendering to God's hands, telling Him, reminding myself, *I trust You.*

Being doctors themselves, Scott and his wife, Mona, knew too much and were scared. "If you need surgery, Dr. Winn is your man," Scott told me. "But realize that we're talking about your brain. Think of the risks— brain damage, blindness, death."

"Scott, I don't want to know those things!" I interrupted, shouting. "They're too frightening."

"Well, at least get another opinion."

Because of our great fear we disregarded the first neurologist's recommendation of immediate surgery. Other opinions meant more tests. Weeks of varying diagnoses.

Trust and terror

During this turmoil I had to keep busy and find new ways to press into God. Outdoors I was captivated by beauty—the morning dew covering everything with diamonds or the wind waltzing through branches. I contemplated each as if it were precious, as if I might never see it again. And throughout each day I concentrated on what I was doing, whom I was with. Being present to these moments made them mine, made them come alive. They became gifts. Like a root forcing itself deeper into fertile soil, I realized my preciousness to God and the tenderness with which He held me. All I needed was to open my eyes and my hands to receive His gifts.

Still, I felt times of terror. In bed at night fear appeared often like a viper coiled before me, its poisonous tongue flicking in my face. "Al, I'm so scared," I'd say, inching toward him.

"Me too." He wrapped his arms around me and again I leaned into God until peace came and I could rest.

We scheduled surgery with Dr. Winn. The occasions of double vision had grown more frequent and my headaches more intense. I felt that I balanced on a knife-edge of trust and uncertainty. Would the aneurysm burst with the doctor I trusted 1,500 miles away?

Our children were holding their breath too. Scott phoned almost daily. Our daughter, Beth Ann, and her husband visited, bringing me the best medicine ever—my first granddaughter! And David, our youngest, away at college, called often. They didn't say "Mom might not be with us much longer," but I knew what they were thinking.

Four days before the surgery was scheduled another neurologist verified its need. Regardless of the outcome, I was at peace. I was not alone.

God seemed to prepare me for death by helping me realize how important my family and friends are to me. I told each one, and made amends where needed. By the time I went to surgery my slate was clean. A wonderful feeling!

"Even if I don't make it," I told Beth Ann, "I'll be OK. And God will be with you just as He's been with me."

"But it wouldn't be the same without you, Mom." The words caught in her throat, and I remembered the nightly talks we'd enjoyed so many years before. Now I was helpless to ease her pain.

On the phone David told me, "All the guys are praying for you, Mom." He paused. "I want to be there for the surgery."

"I know."

Nine-hour suspense

The night before surgery Dr. Winn talked to me about the angiogram they'd done that afternoon. "The aneurysm has changed. It's developed a baby. It's right that we operate in the morning."

"I'll be OK," I told Al, Scott, and Mona. "I'm in good hands." I'll never forget their faces as they kissed me—their stiff smiles, eyes brimming with tears, the squeeze of their hands as I was wheeled away from them into the operating room.

The nine-hour operation began with a lumbar puncture to insert a tube to remove spinal fluid. Another tube was placed in my carotid artery through an incision in my neck to control blood flow when the aneurysm was clipped. A small piece of fat was removed from my abdomen to later cushion the sinus cavity. Then they were ready to open my skull.

After the operation I briefly awoke to see Dr. Winn's face as he repeated slowly, distinctly, "The aneurysm is gone. The aneurysm is gone." After three days of intensive care the crisis was over. I was alive!

Now, one year later, I am well. My senses of taste and smell have lessened. I now eat garlic, onions, and other spicy foods without bother. And I can't smell perfume, fresh paint, or my dog, who used to have an odor like canned tuna fish!

Be a channel for love

One morning, while recuperating at Scott and Mona's, I felt an overwhelming gratitude for God's golden grace, for Dr. Winn, for the love and prayers of family, friends, and people I didn't know. And I had to ask, "Father, what do You want of me?"

His presence filled the room, the goodness like the soft down of feathers falling over and around me. *Love, Carlene. Just love,* He said.

"How? How am I to love?"

By being you. Just be the woman I created you to be.

As I have lived out these weeks of healing, I have come to see that love is not only something we do, but someone we *are,* a channel for His indwelling presence. Just be. Be a woman who walks through the uncertain seasons of life—the letting go of autumn, the bitter cold of winter's loss, the new life and blossom of spring and summer. Knowing that every moment of life is a gift, *just be,* trusting God's love to flow through me because my times—all my times—are in His hands.

~ ~ ~

Carlene Hacker attends Foothills United Methodist Church with her husband. She says that recently she's had a season of germinating—waiting, paying attention, and delighting in small things. She and her husband live in El Cajon, California.

The Power of a Mother's Prayers

Debbonnaire Kovacs

And it came to pass on a certain day that the children of God came together before the Lord, and Satan came among them. When the Lord saw Satan, He said, "Where have you come from?"

Satan answered, "From walking to and fro on my planet, the earth." God did not appear to be overly impressed, so Satan continued boldly, "I have come to publicly declare a grievance. Have you noticed my servant Jason? He is a man after my own heart. Every imagination of his heart is evil continually, and in all things he seeks only to please me. Of course, he thinks merely to please himself, but his understanding will grow with time. He is not interested in You, or in Your rules, or anything about Your kingdom. Is that not so?"

Pain crossed our heavenly Father's face as He nodded. "It is so."

"Now You, O great God of the universe"—Satan gave a mocking bow—"are righteous and just at all times, are You not?"

God looked Satan straight in the eye. "I am."

"And You have given every man, woman, and child on my planet the freedom to choose between You and me," he said with a sneer. "Have You not?"

"I have."

"Then why is it that Your Holy Spirit continually hovers over my servant Jason, whispering to him, pleading with him, nagging him to join Your side? Every time I try to get him to do something for me, my angels first have to fight off Your angels. You are invading his thoughts, interfering with his choices, and making his life miserable! By what right do You do these things?"

"Jason may be your servant now, but I still love him," answered God.

"I don't care," Satan snarled. "You gave him a choice, and *he chose me!* You are breaking Your own laws!"

There was a moment of shocked silence in the throne room, then a surge of movement among the angels around the throne. God lifted His hand, and the room grew still.

Very quietly God asked, "Have you noticed My servant Anne? Anne is a woman after My own heart, and every thought of her heart is only to please Me. Yet I notice you are always whispering to her, ready to attack her. My angels continually fight yours for her safety."

Satan smiled. *"I never promised to play fair!"*

God let it pass. "When Anne came to Me, she and I made a covenant together. She would be My child. She would love Me, trust Me, look to Me for guidance, and stay close to My side every day of her life. She would place all that she is, has, or ever hopes for in My hands. I would be her Father. I would keep her safe from you and all your snares. I would care for her, teach her, and love her with all My heart. And I would answer every prayer she prayed within My will and in My Son's name.

"Since that day Anne has asked Me for many things. Some I have refused, since they were not in My will for her. But every day of our life together Anne has asked Me for one thing above all others. She has asked Me for the life of her son Jason. Anne prays with persistence, with thanksgiving, and without fear, because she trusts Me. I have given her My word."

Suddenly God stood up, and Satan cringed and fell back. It made him furious, but he couldn't help it as the voice of the Father, like flames of fire, flowed over his head. "My covenant with My daughter Anne was signed by My right hand, sealed by the blood of My Son, and delivered by the eternal presence of My Holy Spirit in her life! *That* is My legal right over your client. *Be gone!"*

Satan fled. The cheers of the angels sped his passing.

~ ~ ~

Debbonnaire Kovacs, author of the book *Gardens of the Soul,* enjoys gardening—of course—raising sheep, spinning wool, and weaving. She and her husband have three children.

Cover Your Eyes
While We Fast-Forward

Kim Peckham

Many things in life seem like a good idea until you try them. Fat-free potato chips, for example.

It might also seem like a good idea to invite your church friends over on a long winter evening to enjoy a video. Let me share a few words of advice: DON'T EVEN THINK ABOUT IT! In my experience, the trip to Blockbusters almost never has a happy ending.

The first hint of trouble comes when you try to settle on a video everyone will watch. I mean, the last movie you could get Adventists to agree on was *The Sound of Music*.

So choosing a movie becomes a delicate negotiation, with proposals and counter-proposals that resemble a church board trying to decide on the carpet color for the new sanctuary.

"How 'bout this one?"

"I've seen it."

"How 'bout this one?"

"Nah, I saw the whale in person, and he's got a big head."

These negotiations get particularly tough because men and woman have completely different tastes in movies. Women want bittersweet stories of love triumphing against impossible odds. Men want bittersweet stories of a man with a gun triumphing against impossible odds.

The women in the group will vote for a movie like *Sarah Plain and Tall*. "No thanks," the men will say. "Normally we love to watch movies about plain women who write letters about their cats, but tonight we'll just sit out in the car and listen to the ball game."

If you add children to the viewer mix, well, you suddenly realize how important it is for youngsters to have an early bedtime. Say about 6:00 p.m. Otherwise you're going to end up watching *Babe*—the sheep-herding pig—one more time.

You might be tempted to skip the negotiations and just pick out a movie you want to watch. That's a bad idea because that leaves no one to share the blame when the movie ambushes you with a scene that makes everyone in the room cringe.

I'm always getting ambushed. About 30 minutes after I put the video in the player, the cold chill of embarrassment starts creeping up my spine. The actors are spouting language I haven't heard since the time I went Ingathering at a construction site. Or I am witnessing a murder in as much detail as possible without actually attaching a tiny camera to the bullet. Or the leading lady is participating with the leading man in an activity which, according to large parts of Leviticus and 1 Corinthians, they should not.

One time I gathered a houseful of friends—two of whom were local el-ders—in front of the TV, and the star actress arrived on the screen much like Eve makes her first appearance in *The Bible Story*, only without the chaste positioning of a rosebush.

There's nothing you can do to stop this. You can't get all the actors together beforehand and say, "Look, I'm having some respectable friends over, and I would appreciate it if everyone would keep their clothes on. And by the way—all of you with speaking parts—let me explain the third commandment."

In theory, the rating system should help me avoid embarrassment, but I can't figure it out. I suspect that the MPAA rating assigned to each movie involves someone's pet monkey and a box of Scrabble tiles.

Once I thought I had a clever plan to entertain without corrupting anyone's morals. I determined I would find an old movie—a classic from those innocent days when they didn't even need a rating system. The house was filled with friends when I presented a Cary Grant comedy that co-starred two elderly and innocent-looking women. Well, it turned out that the dear ladies were poisoning men and burying them in the basement.

Why do movies so often ambush us with words and images that make us cringe? Perhaps it's because Hollywood doesn't have a lot in common with Christians. I'm afraid they think that a family value refers to the money you save when you buy the big box of Cheerios.

Once, when Paul was trying to straighten out the Corinthians, he asked them, "What does a believer have in common with an unbeliever?"

And sometimes when I watch a video with my Christian friends, I realize that we don't have much in common with Hollywood at all. And the sooner we push the "stop" button, the sooner we'll have a happy ending.

~ ~ ~

Kim Peckham, director of periodical advertising for the Review and Herald, and his wife, Lori, turn off their TV in their home in West Virginia.

Arms of Love

I looked around me at the familiar living room and realized I hadn't been there in months. It surprised me. Sally was one of my best friends, yet I had shut her out of my life, hoping she wouldn't find out what I was doing.

Several months before, I'd determined I didn't want to have anything more to do with God. To prove it, I decided to run away. And run I did. I ran fast, I ran hard, and I ran blindly. I got involved in things that even now make me shake my head in wonder and gratitude that I survived.

I blamed God for an ugly situation that had left me hurting and wanting to be loved. To get even with Him, I found love in whatever form I could. My activities did satisfy me, but only for a moment. The morning after was always waiting for me. And each morning after left me empty, pushing me to run even faster to fill the void.

So there I sat in Sally's living room after months of emptiness, wanting to be loved so badly it wrenched my very soul. I longed to open up to her about my pain, but I was terrified that if she found out what I'd done—what I was doing—even she wouldn't love me anymore. So I tried my best to pretend that everything was all right.

We chitchatted about everyday things, and gradually the wall I'd built around myself began to erode. She chipped away at it, and I didn't even realize what was happening. Then she said something—I wish I could remember what it was—and the pressure inside me exploded like a geyser.

Sally wept, too

I sat there like a blob of Jell-O and sobbed out the whole sordid story. Everything. I couldn't have stopped if I'd tried. At last all the deep, dark uglies had poured out, and I sat silently, waiting for my judgment.

Sally is a close friend of Jesus. Since I figured Jesus had already written me off, I put two and two together and thought Sally would too. I slowly, hesitantly raised my eyes, waiting to hear the condemnation I knew I deserved. But instead of lecturing me, pointing out my terrible sin, and telling me that I'd better mend my ways, I saw tears in her eyes. Sally wept with me, feeling my pain, loving me through my hurt.

She reached over, hugged me tightly, and whispered, "Sharon, I still love you. I understand *completely* how you feel. I know Jesus knows and understands, and most of all, I know He loves you too."

All of a sudden I believed He did love me. After all those months of being dead sure He'd hate me for what I was doing, I felt hope. Why? Because one of His close friends loved me the way He does—totally, completely, unconditionally.

How could I keep on running from such a God?

~ ~ ~

Sharon Garcia was a full-time student of organizational management when this story was written. She and her husband, David, enjoy their four cats.

The Golden Moment

June Strong

One morning, my errands completed, I stopped in at the local library. It's my favorite place in our small city, but I seldom have time to spend there, and a leisurely hour was a rare treat.

In my purse I keep a list of books that I'm hoping to read, so my first priority was to track down *The Search for Significance,* by Robert McGee. With it safely tucked under my arm, I proceeded to the new book section. Because most of my reading is either work-related or for my own spiritual edification, I seldom select one of the new titles, but I do browse among them. Occasionally, I succumb to a biography or some other tantalizing topic.

Once I've exhausted the new books, I head for the gardening shelves. The best for last! I have read nearly every book there, but I run my finger along the spines, hoping for a new title. Aha! A nice big coffee-table glossy by Penelope Hobhouse, full-color illustrations on every page. And with Penelope behind the pen, the text will be as glorious as the photography. As I've come to be more knowledgeable about plants, I enjoy going through such a book and attempting to identify all the flowers in those famous old British gardens. What I usually discover is that I still have much to learn, but it's a lovely game. So I tuck *Country Gardner* under my arm too and head for the check-out desk.

On rare occasions, maybe once each winter, my daughter, Amy, and I spend an afternoon at the library. We don't waste time searching the stacks for elusive titles, but head instead straight for the reading room. There, on winter days, a fire blazes on the hearth and we wander along the racks selecting choice specialty magazines to which we'd never subscribe, but which we fully enjoy. Sinking into a soft leather couch, we settle in for a totally luxurious afternoon.

There's something about that dark-paneled, fire-lit room—so cozy, so serene, so removed from the hurly-burly of life—that projects an aura of timelessness, of some bygone leisurely age. Beyond its stone walls, of course, traffic ebbs and flows, and all the duties I'm neglecting crouch like predators, but we relax and read and share whispered discoveries, my daughter and I. And when we leave, something good has ended. We both know it, and tuck it away like a choice treasure in a memory box.

Rest in the quiet

One morning when I completed my devotions, it occurred to me that those moments with God that I'd just spent were a lot like our winter afternoons at the library. There was the same entering into warmth and peace and seclusion from a demanding, raucous world. The same awareness that the golden moment must be hugged to one's heart and carried out into life like a glowing coal. But there the comparison ends, for the healing in one's rendezvous with God cannot be found in any reading room. And there's a "foreverness" about it that contrasts sharply with life's secular experiences.

Come into the presence of the Lord. Be healed, nurtured, and taught. Rest in the quiet. Only then open the doors of the new morning.

~ ~ ~

June Strong, author of *Mindy* and *Song of Eve,* was a speaker, writer, and columnist for many years. She and her husband live in beautiful upstate New York.

"May I Serve You?"

Jo Anne Chitwood Nowack

I stood in the corner of the room watching as women filed past me, laughing and talking in excited little huddles. It was Communion Sabbath, and the air seemed alive with spiritual energy. The pastor had just given a particularly stirring message highlighting the meaning of the sacraments and the privilege of following Jesus' example when He washed the disciples' feet before that special Passover service so long ago. When the congregation divided for foot washing—the men to one room and the women to another—I had followed a giggling group of teenage girls to the room the women would use.

I moved farther back into my corner with a heartfelt sigh. The pain and frustration of a long, hard week pressed on my mind. I knew God loved me; it just didn't feel as though He was there for me. Everyone else seemed so excited and spiritually "together," paired with the partner of her choice. I felt like the odd woman out.

Father, I prayed silently, *this old feeling of being all alone, far away from You and everyone else, isn't much fun. I know You love me, and I know I'm never really alone. Please give me the faith to believe it, even when I feel so lonely. And could You send me someone to share this service with?*

I watched as women filed into the room two by two, one sitting down in a chair, the other filling a small plastic basin with warm water to wash her partner's feet. The murmur of soft, flowing background music and of voices praying low filled the room with a sense of peace. I edged closer to the door, feeling my loneliness ebbing away. It was then that I saw her.

My partner

She hobbled through the doorway, an old leather purse clutched in one hand and a cane in the other. A tattered, hand-knit sweater hung on her bent shoulders, and her snow-white hair peeked out from under a worn wool scarf. A greeter standing just inside the door stepped up to her, slipped an arm around her, and asked if she had a partner.

"No," she said, her voice quavering.

"Well, you just stand over here in this corner until we can find someone to be your partner," the greeter said, gently guiding her toward where I stood. The old woman wore an expression of quiet resignation, as if she were accustomed to being shuffled off into corners by a younger, more energetic generation.

At that moment I stepped forward and reached out to touch the woman's shoulder. She looked up in surprise. "I don't have a partner," I said.

Her face broke into a beautiful smile and her dark eyes twinkled. "Well, then," she said, "may I serve you?"

I started for the table where the basins of warm water were being distributed, but the woman held out her hand to stop me. She motioned to a nearby chair. "I'll get the water," she said. "You sit there."

As I sat on the edge of the cold metal chair, I watched her trembling hands reach for the basin and towel and carry them back to me. Then she knelt, placing the basin in front of me, and gently washed and dried my feet. When she had finished, I traded places with her. As I did, I studied the wrinkled old hands folded serenely in her lap and the bent and crooked feet that I held in my hands. I thought of the many fevered brows those hands must have soothed and the miles those tired old feet had traveled in the service of her Master.

A sense of awe and reverence welled up in my heart as I realized what a privilege it was just to be in her presence. When we finished, I whispered, "Could we have a prayer together?" Before I could say another word, she placed her cheek next to mine and began to pray. She asked for a blessing on my life and on the others in the room, she praised God for His goodness, and she thanked Him for another day of life.

Tears welled up in my eyes as I listened to her conversation with Someone she knew so very well. I was in the presence of spiritual greatness, and I felt it keenly. After she said "Amen," she put her arms around me, hugging me close. "God bless you, dear," she said, and turned to go.

"But wait," I stammered. "I didn't introduce myself. My name is JoAnne. What is yours?"

A radiant smile lit up her face. She leaned toward me, reaching out to touch my hand. "My name is Faith."

~ ~ ~

JoAnne Chitwood Nowack, mother of three, loves hiking, bicycling, and horseback riding. She and her husband work with grief recovery.

Live Dangerously, Sleep on a Mattress

Kim Peckham

According to the statistic that I just made up, 38 percent of women feel that their lives are boring. Well, no wonder. We live in an age when there are simply not enough things that can eat you.

In the old days, when Mrs. Daniel Boone left the house, she had a good chance of meeting a bear. That made her life much more exciting than yours or mine. Even a church finance committee can be thrilling if you're anxious about making it home afterward without wringing bear saliva out of your skirt.

But today in North America there's nothing that will eat you. You can travel far and wide, and never be in danger from any of God's creatures—unless you count the bacteria in those interstate restrooms.

So we're living in a country that's as safe as a parked Volvo, and frankly, we will perish from boredom if we don't discover some element of danger in our lives. That's why we can be grateful for the Internet.

Take the example of my friend Larissa. She had a fairly ho-hum existence until she came across an Internet site that exposed the dangers of her office computer. According to the Web site, computer monitors send off some kind of death ray that will turn your eyes into Hostess Snowballs. Suddenly going to work has an exciting sense of peril for Larissa, and her donations to National Camps for the Blind have increased dramatically.

I recently came across a Web site that added a bracing sense of danger to my holiday celebrations. This site alerted me to the hazards of spruce Christmas trees. Apparently spruce needles are so sharp that if children should accidentally brush against the tree—mothers, you may want to avert your eyes to avoid the horror I am about to describe—they will experience a painful pricking sensation on exposed areas of their skin!

Of course, the Internet story that has created the greatest thrill for us all is the e-mail about the missing kidneys. I'm referring to the story about the guy who, after a night on the town, wakes up in a tub of ice with a neatly sewn incision on his back and a note around his neck saying that his kidneys have been stolen.

I am somewhat suspicious about this story, because the kidney thieves seem very considerate. First they stitch up the wounds, then they leave a helpful note suggesting the victim call 911. I'm surprised they didn't leave a prescription for antibiotics and an appointment card for a post-op visit.

Perhaps you've also noticed that television news shows try to whip up a sense of danger in everyday life. I tuned in the other night to hear this teaser: "Are you sleeping on something dangerous? Your bed could turn into a ball of fire!" The local Fox station thought it would be amusing to run this story on the 10:00 news, just before their viewers tucked themselves in for the night.

Well, I had to watch. A very serious investigative reporter demonstrated how your mattress and bed linen will catch fire if—surprise—you leave an open flame underneath the bed. So there you have it: another reason not to invite the Pathfinders to have their wienie roast in your bedroom.

On this earth we're pretty safe, but never perfectly safe. There is always enough danger to give us a thrill of fear and a rush of anxiety—which may be why Jesus put a few lines in the Sermon on the Mount about not being anxious about tomorrow. He seemed to know that even in a time when lions or bears aren't roaming the streets, people can still get eaten alive by worry.

~ ~ ~

Kim Peckham's wife, Lori, refuses to use cell phones because she doesn't want the electromagnetic waves close to her head, but she uses a 1,200-watt hair dryer. Kim and Lori have one son, Reef.

God's Soft Touch

Jennifer Bonney

It's Mother's Day. Once again I've spent the weekend hearing comparisons to the woman of Proverbs and sermons on the uniqueness and awesome responsibilities of mothers. I feel appreciated and despondent at the same time. After all, how can the mother whom the pastor describes in all her virtue have anything to do with *me?* I'm struggling just to keep my three wiggly preschoolers in the pew and semi-quiet.

I hear the long litany of commitments and achievements, and quite frankly, I'm overwhelmed. Summarizing a mother's lifetime responsibilities in 30 minutes leaves me sitting with a mountain on my shoulders. Stop already! I can handle only one day at a time, and so far my only accomplishment has been to get my children to church on time, clean and dressed. My weary heart says that this is supposed to encourage me, but all this recognition is getting me down.

The next day as I pondered these thoughts, God stepped in and showed me a verse I'd read many times but never really seen. I found it, of all places, in the Sunday morning paper.

"He shall feed his flock like a shepherd: he shall gather the lambs with his arm, and carry them in his bosom, and shall gently lead those that are with young" (Isa. 40:11, KJV).

Wow! He will *gently* lead those with young. That one phrase speaks of understanding and compassion. He understands how overwhelming my job can be. He empathizes with our frustrations and so is gentle with us. He doesn't say that He'll wait for us until motherhood is over. No, He's there, always present, but gentle.

Gentle with our frazzled emotions.

Gentle with our tired bodies.
Gentle with our aching hearts.
Gentle with our vulnerability.
Gentle with our desire to do it all and be the best we can be.
Gentle. Gently He holds us. Gently He is there.
Never pushing—we see too much of that.
Never yelling—we hear that too.
Never demanding—our days are full of demands.

Just gently leading, providing the very thing we long for and never seem to find, a gentle hand, a direction to go.

Now I do not need to feel unequal to the woman of Proverbs 31. I have no need to hang my head. My Shepherd is leading me, gently.

~ ~ ~

Jennifer Bonney was a home-schooling mom of three when she write this article. She understands the comfort of being gently led by the Good Shepherd.

A Woman of Spirit

By faith Rahab, the Jericho prostitute, welcomed the Israelite spies and escaped the destruction that came on those who refused to trust God" (see Heb. 11:31).

"So here's what I want you to do, God helping you: Take your everyday, ordinary life—your sleeping, eating, going-to-work, and walking-around life—and place it before God as an offering. . . . Fix your attention on God. You'll be changed from the inside out. Readily recognize what he wants from you, and quickly respond to it" (Rom. 12:1-3, Message).*

I knew I was in trouble the moment she walked into my office. Her stern look of disapproval, the rigidity of her body, and the stiff way she sat holding her purse on her knees all told me that this was not a friendly call to affirm her pastor.

"There's a woman coming here who's a disgrace to the Adventist Church," began Mrs. Snipe, her words cutting through the tension that stretched between us. "She sits on the front pew every week," she added as if I wouldn't know immediately on whom her venom was being sprayed. "She looks like a prostitute, and my husband and I want to know what you plan to do about it!"

I sat quietly a moment, collecting my thoughts. Then before I could open my mouth to speak Mrs. Snipe sprang to her feet. "You better tell her to take off the makeup and fake pearls before she comes to church again!" she hissed.

I tried to reply, but she interrupted, biting each word and spitting it my direction. "If you don't do something immediately, my husband and I will transfer our membership to another church!" She flung her head back

73

so hard I thought her neck had snapped, but it was only the sound of the door slamming shut as she stormed out of my office.

Janet (not her real name) was, in fact, a prostitute. Reared in a Catholic family in Boston, as she entered her teen years she nominally accepted her family's faith. But something went terribly wrong. While still a teenager she became promiscuous, and eventually a prostitute. Her life went from bad to worse, and after many unsuccessful attempts to leave her shameful lifestyle she decided to commit suicide. In her troubled mind she felt that she had no real choice, that her only way out was death at her own hands. At that time almost daily local papers ran photographs of yet another young Massachusetts woman who'd been brutally murdered by an unapprehended serial killer of prostitutes. Janet decided to kill herself rather than to live in degradation and fear.

The day she planned to end her life a stranger visited the massage parlor where she worked. Strangely, he insisted that he was not there to seek sex, but to save her so that he could marry her one day. He told her to find a church that kept the seventh-day Sabbath because, he said, "they are the only people I know who can help you get out of the life you now have." Then he left.

His arrogant intrusion angered her. Who did he think he was, bursting in like that, telling her she needed to change? And yet she couldn't help being curious about his challenge. She reasoned that she had nothing to lose, so she began searching the yellow pages under "churches," calling one after another, asking if they kept the Sabbath. She had no idea what "keep the Sabbath" meant, and finally an impatient minister—put off by her questions—told her, "Go talk to the Adventists." It was then that she called the Boston Temple Seventh-day Adventist Church, which I pastored.

I remember that first telephone contact. By her tone and choice of words, I thought it was a crank call. By the time she asked how much we charged for Bible studies, I was sure it was. When I insisted that we meet and talk personally, she abruptly hung up. I looked at the telephone receiver and said, "Well, that's that!"

But a half hour later on that overcast April afternoon I saw Janet for the first time. I was thankful that I, and not my male associate pastor, answered the knock on the church door. It seemed to me that the taxi driver hesitated to leave. He leaned toward the passenger's window, peering at the person he thought had ordered a prostitute, delivered like a pizza, to the church office. I realized more than ever that there are some definite, unexpected advantages in being a female pastor. And I welcomed Janet loudly to her first Bible study—for the benefit of the nosy cab driver, of course.

Janet was a sight to behold. Thick, long, blond hair cascaded in a mop of frizzy curls down her shoulders and back. The shocking color of her blood-red lips matched the polish on her long, curving fingernails. Her eyes darted back and forth nervously from pools painted with wide, black lines and highlighted by bright-green eyeshadow. And our hallway light danced in prisms from her dangling lantern-shaped earrings. They clicked back and forth every time she moved her head. Her black leather skirt—just about the size of a wide belt—hardly covered her hips. Her long legs were encased in black stockings. She wore pencil-heeled shoes.

"You the person I spoke to a few minutes ago?" she asked cautiously.

"Yes," I said with a smile, welcoming her quickly into the office. I was careful not to stare at her appearance.

"I'd like to speak to the priest," she said defensively.

"I'm the pastor," I said.

"But you're a woman!" she exclaimed, slapping her hand across her mouth as if to force the words back down her throat. And then we sat down together, and for several hours Janet poured out the gory details of a promising life derailed by sin, and the sorrow and desperation that led her to decide to take her own life. I shared the gospel of God's favor with her and had the privilege of leading her to accept Christ as her personal Saviour. At the end of our session I gave Janet her first Bible, showed her how to read her name in Romans 5 and 8 and to learn the disciples' prayer in Matthew 6.

Janet began attending our church that very week and did not miss a Bible study or Sabbath service throughout the time she lived in Boston. I didn't tell her how to dress, but noticed that the first Sabbath she came to church she wore a knee-length dress and a lot less makeup and jewelry. She walked down the aisle and sat on the front pew so that she, as she told me, "wouldn't miss a single thing."

Following our church's mission statement, "to inspire discipleship in Christ, to function as an extended family, to minister in our neighborhood, and to nurture all God's children," neither pastor nor members act as clothes police to people coming to church. We accept everyone just as they come to Jesus, that His Holy Spirit might transform them into His likeness. And the Spirit has consistently and successfully done this during my six-year tenure at the Boston Temple. So imagine my surprise when one of our leaders, Mrs. Snipe, paid me that infamous visit. I felt badly that she couldn't rejoice with the angels in heaven over the restoration of her prodigal sister who was eagerly sacrificing everything to be transformed into a daughter of the most high God.

But Mrs. Snipe and her family were not comfortable attending a church they claimed had abandoned the traditions of Adventism to allow people such as Janet to come just as they are. And a few months after their departure Janet shocked our congregation once again. One memorable Sabbath we all failed to recognize her at first glance. Gone were the long, flowing tresses, the dangling jewelry, the finger rings, and the heavy makeup. Even the defiant curl of her lips and the cheap cologne of the streets had been replaced by the soft smile of grace and the scent of salvation. At the same time she rejoiced in her engagement to that stranger who kept his promise and with whom she was now very much in love and later married. One Sabbath I baptized her along with six other candidates before a congregation celebrating her miraculous transformation.

Janet has since moved to another state, where she serves as Sabbath school superintendent and teacher. A year ago Janet became a full-time undergraduate student pursuing a degree in education. I thank her for allowing me to share her story, for she is truly a "woman of Spirit." She returns to Boston regularly to "walk the streets again," as she likes to tease me with a smile and wink. I'm glad she does, because she spends her time sharing her newfound freedom in Christ with her former friends. Sometimes she spends hours holding drug-addicted women dying with AIDS in her arms, singing songs of praise to them, praying with them, and reciting the precious scriptures that promise their deliverance. She showers them with God's unconditional love and the assurance of a place for them in God's kingdom.

Last Christmas, as we hugged in the foyer after church, Janet whispered, "Pastor, I believe the Lord is calling me into the ministry. Do you think the seminary is ready for 'Rahab's resurrection'?"

"Yes!" I shouted confidently. "Yes, oh, yes."

~ ~ ~

This story is taken from Pastor Hyveth Williams' book, *Will I Ever Learn?* © 1996 by the Review and Herald. Williams, a native Jamaican, grew up in London, England. She is the first female senior pastor in the SDA church, currently serving in Loma Linda, California.

Nobody Loves Me

Aali Butler

On a Friday evening just before sunset, I sat in my living room after a full day of running errands, doing ministry, and fighting Los Angeles traffic. As I sat in silence, trying not to think of anything else that needed to be done, the devil invaded my privacy with a thought so dark that it could have pushed me into deep depression, if not death.

"No man thinks of you as special," he whispered. "There is not one man on the face of the earth that's thinking about you. Who loves you? You're all alone. You've got no one." I could almost hear him laugh. "Look at you," he taunted. "You're not loved. Nobody loves you. *Nobody!*"

His words engulfed me, almost taking my breath away. But I quickly recognized whose voice I heard in my head, and I knew what to do to combat his attacks. Heading to my music cabinet, I found one of my favorite praise worship tapes. I popped it into my boom box and turned up the volume, drowning out the silence and voices that sought to destroy my peaceful day. The music was soothing, satisfying, inviting me to the throne of God. I didn't need to sit in my quiet room, attacked and alone. Jesus invited me to join Him and I did.

That night, exhausted after ministering to another single female friend by telephone for two and a half hours, I retired early. At 4:00 a.m. I was awakened. I can only tell you that Jesus came to me in my room. The dark room was filled with the light of His presence. He talked with me, He held me, and He affirmed me for what seemed to be eternity. During this time I watched Him move around the room. Then He went to the bookshelf and knelt down to reach for something in a stack of papers on the bottom shelf.

"Is this what you were looking for?" He asked in a humble, kind voice. He continued to assure me of His love, His concern for my every need, and His willingness always to be by my side.

The phone rang at 7:02, interrupting my special morning with Jesus. It was a women's ministry leader following through on an assignment for our upcoming women's retreat. I talked with her a few minutes; then, as I hung up the phone, my mind went back to my early-morning experience with Jesus.

A *dream, only a dream*, I reasoned. But as I stepped out of bed, my eyes fell on the bookshelf and stack of papers Jesus had touched during our interlude. *No*, I thought, *don't start searching again for that document; it's Sabbath, and you'll be late for church.* I had spent more than three hours on Friday frantically tearing through my room searching for an important document that I'd misplaced.

But a strong impression led me to the bookcase. I lifted the folders and went directly to a small stack of loose papers. As I pulled the papers toward me, my eyes saw the "lost" document—right on the top, just as Jesus left it for me during His visit.

I felt the light of His presence once again in my life. No one—not even Satan himself—can take it away. My Lord and Saviour dispelled darkness, restored my joy, and made Himself real to me. *I am loved!*

~ ~ ~

Sali Butler, at the time of this writing, was an Adventist Volunteer teaching in Korea. Now back in North America, she is an active leader in both prayer ministries and women's ministries.

The Prayer Mop

Felita Callahan

Oh Lord," I grumbled, "when is it all going to be over?" I angrily thrust the mop into the bucket again and took a few more quick swipes at my kitchen floor.

I was on a rollercoaster of despair and joy—and despair was winning. Juggling the responsibilities of wife, working mother of a 4-year-old and 9-month-old, with baby number three on the way, I was simply overwhelmed. I made a few more anger-driven swipes at the dirty floor and thought *I'm just so tired and weary.*

Shoving the bucket, I glared resentfully as the murky gray water sloshed over the side and splattered across the floor. *I hate to mop!* my mind shouted. Resentment washed over me in a wave of bitterness, draining the last of my energy. I abruptly thrust the mop aside. It clattered against the cabinet as I slowly slumped against the sink.

I was ashamed of my thoughts and began to pray, "Lord, this is ridiculous. I don't know why I'm acting like this. Please help me." In that instant a text from my child's Sabbath school lesson immediately came to mind: "Whatsoever you do, do all to the glory of God."

The glory of mopping

Lord, how can I glorify You by mopping my floor? I stood for a moment while thoughts flew like little birds inside my head. I looked at my floor—textured, cream-colored 6-inch squares. A stillness slowly began to settle in me as I repeated the scripture.

"OK, Lord," I said aloud, "I'm going to mop square by square and pray for my church family by name."

I emptied the bucket, refilled it with clean water, and began mopping again. As I swished the mop back and forth across the first square, I silently prayed. *Merciful Father, lay Your healing hands on Sister Turner. Lift her up and grant her Your healing mercies as she recovers from her surgery.*

Swish, swish.

Loving Father, comfort the Kelly family in their time of loss. Dry their tears and mend their broken hearts. Help them cling to Your promise of hope and eternal life.

Swish, swish, swish.

Creator God, thank You for the precious baby You've blessed the Richardsons with. Grant them wisdom, patience, and strength as they embark on the parenthood journey.

Swish, swish, swish. . . .

Square by square my kitchen was transformed. Prayer by prayer my soul was transformed. As I emptied the bucket praising the Lord, I was once again overwhelmed. This time it was with a sense of awe at the power of God. Such a simple instruction . . . Do all to the glory of God, but such an awesome result—a transformed kitchen and life.

I chuckled to myself. A prayer closet? Yes.

But whoever heard of a prayer mop?

~ ~ ~

Felita Callahan, from Humble, Texas, is a home health physical therapist. She enjoys reading, writing, and Tai Chi. She and her husband, Milton, have five children.

Interested Party

Gina Lee

When I first saw the cat at the animal shelter, I wanted to take her home with me. She was so friendly that it seemed we already belonged together. She had a funny white stripe around her mouth that made her look as though she was always smiling. Her coat was a gray-and-white tuxedo affair. I knew she was going to be my cat the minute I touched her.

I told the attendant that I wanted her. Unfortunately, there was a three-day wait. Previously I'd picked out a lovely little longhaired cat, but by the end of the waiting period he had already been put to sleep. The workers at the shelter told me that when a cat gets sick they put it to sleep right away. Knowing how easily stressed cats catch diseases, I was afraid this cat—my cat—wouldn't make it past the holding period either. Now I begged for her life, telling the attendant that I didn't care if the cat became sick. I wanted her, no matter what.

The attendant said that would be no problem. She would just mark the cat's card for me. She took out a pen and wrote "I.P." on the cage's card.

"I.P.?" I asked. "What's that mean?"

"Interested Party," she told me. "If the vet knows there's an interested party, he will go ahead and treat the cat."

Such a simple act—two letters on a card, and the cat would live!

I named her Gilah, which is Hebrew for "joy." When the waiting period was up, I redeemed her from the shelter hospital. She had, in fact, become very ill, but because I was an I.P. she had been allowed to live. Eleven years later she is still my joy.

We all have at least one Interested Party—Jesus Christ. He cared enough to write "I.P." on our cards—only He wrote it not in ink, but in blood. He is willing to do whatever it takes to save us. He is the one who offers us life eternal. Because there is an Interested Party, we have a future, and a chance for something more—to become Christ's joy.

Dear Lord, I feel as though we belong together—You and I. I want You for my Forever Master. I praise You for being my Interested Party—I have no other future. You are my hope for today.

~ ~ ~

Gina Lee has written more than 500 stories, articles, and poems. When not writing, she enjoys working at the public library and caring for her four cats. This article first appeared in the women's devotional *Fabric of Faith*.

God's Grace and Gleaming Dentures

Sally Pierson Dillon

With a flourish I finished brushing the last pair of dentures and set them gleaming with the other 31 sets on the sterile towel spread on the treatment room counter. I stood back with a sigh of satisfaction to survey my work.

"What on earth have you done?" cried my charge nurse from the doorway.

I looked up smiling with calm accomplishment. I had just started working as a nurse's aide for a nursing agency. It was important that I be fast and efficient to represent the agency and to be asked back. I was determined to be perfect. After making initial rounds, doing the vital signs and bedchecks, I organized my night. I'd passed out clean linens for the morning, and all my patients were snoring gently when I decided to clean all of their dentures. Too often the false teeth got a perfunctory rinsing and dumping in a cup. Tonight they would receive the scrubbing of their lives! Tomorrow everyone's smiles would sparkle, and the unit would be a better place because I had been there that night.

"I've cleaned everyone's teeth," I said proudly.

"So I see," she replied. "How can you tell whose teeth are whose?"

Suddenly my feeling of accomplishment was replaced by a sinking sensation in the pit of my stomach. Thirty-two sets of teeth—smiling so happily on the counter—now seemed to be leering at me. There were 42 patients on our floor. The teeth of 32 of them sat unmarked and unidentified before me. So much for my fantasies of perfection!

By 9:00 a.m. the following morning I was exhausted—and 10 patients had their own dentures in their mouths. The other sets of teeth continued to leer from the counter as I tried them in one patient after another, cleaning each set again for the next "fitting." My charge nurse, who was still there too, observed my dejection and fatigue and said, "Go home, Sally. You made a mistake, and you've done your best to make it better. Don't stay up beating yourself. Go home and rest. I'll take care of this."

Forgiven

I went home overwhelmed with feelings of failure, and fearful that I'd never be able to work there again.

I got a call that afternoon asking me to return. They wanted me back! I went to work hesitantly, expecting to find the patients crabby and hungry, having been unable to eat properly all day. I guessed that the charge nurse had called me back to finish finding the right mouths for all those teeth. But what I found was a quiet floor, everyone tucked in bed, and a friendly charge nurse. Everyone had their teeth back, and no one mentioned the horrible, embarrassing thing that had happened the night before.

Finally I couldn't stand it any longer. "Why did you ask for me back after last night?" I asked. "I know that what I did probably cost you your whole day's sleep, and I feel so bad!"

"I know," she said with a tired smile, "but after seeing what it cost, you'll never do that again, and a little grace is good for everyone."

Unfortunately, that night on 5-south reflects my spiritual life sometimes. No matter how perfect I plan to be, and how busy a do-gooder my Martha mentality pushes me to be, I make some major mistakes. But I do learn from them. And when I look at what my mistakes cost, and remember the price God paid for them, I find an overwhelming incentive not to make the same mistake again.

I get the same feelings of forgiveness and love and unconditional acceptance from Him as I did from my charge nurse that fateful night.

And she was right. A little grace *is* good for everyone.

~ ~ ~

Sally Pierson Dillon enjoys looking at things from a different angle. Maybe that's why she got herself into trouble with all those teeth! Sally, a prolific writer, is the author of a 3-book series, *War of the Ages*, published by the Review and Herald Publishing Association.

One Big Mama

A nyone with a thimbleful of common sense would tell you that you don't turn your life over to a perfect stranger in New York City after dark. But this is precisely the impression I received in response to one of the shortest, most frantic prayers I've ever uttered.

I was a brand-new émigré to the United States from my native Trinidad, and as green as the savannah grass I'd left behind. I'd never been away from home unchaperoned—not even to social church functions. One of my four trusty brothers had always been around to ensure my safety. Yet here I was in New York City, a gawky prep-school grad, trying to establish my independence and earn my way through college.

I worked days, attended evening classes at a community college, and averaged five to six hours of sleep a night. I had the unwise habit of compensating for the sleep deficiency by falling asleep on the subway every night and dozing through the long, tedious ride from Manhattan to my stop in Brooklyn.

About 11:00 one unforgettable evening I paid my last token and boarded the train that would take me close to Albermarle Road, where I rented a room in the home of a Christian family. My pockets were completely empty, for I'd spent my loose change on snack foods. Since I was headed home, the wisdom of retaining at least a quarter for an emergency phone call did not occur to me.

As usual, I made a pillow out of my book bag, propped my shoulders up against a corner, folded my arms, and promptly fell sound asleep. The subway car had been half full when I boarded the train in Manhattan. Sometime later I was awakened by the jolt of the train lurching to a stop.

I looked around. The car was empty.

Lost and scared

I grabbed my books and rushed out the door, but the place was unfamiliar. With a shock I realized that I'd slept beyond my stop and had reached the end of the line for that train. To catch the uptown train, I'd have to leave the subway station and walk or drive to an uptown station.

There were two major obstacles. First, I was penniless, and second, the platform was deserted and I had no idea of exactly where I was.

As I cautiously began walking toward the exit stairway I saw him. Positioned off the side of the stairway, he crouched like a giant tomcat, his hooded eyes measuring my steps. I'd read of subway victims whose bodies were undiscovered for hours. No one would hear my cry for help, and I had nowhere to go but forward.

Fear pinched the back of my neck, and the prayer that I uttered would make sense only to God. "Help me . . . my long legs," I gasped, now within eight feet of the man. His body coiled, ready to pounce. I am six feet tall, but he seemed to me like a Goliath.

In that instant energy surged through me, and I took a sudden flying leap past him and up the stairs. From the corner of my eye I saw him swivel, ready to follow. Then he saw the same person who looked kindly down at me as I raced to the top of the stairs.

She was a rotund black woman with a broad-rimmed hat framing a chubby face, and a bosom like two cantaloupes under her sturdy cotton dress. I will never forget her, this motherly stranger. "Child, are you lost? Follow me." She didn't wait for my answer, and strangely enough, I didn't hesitate, but followed.

There was no further conversation between us. I remember her huffing and puffing as we climbed the flight of steps to get to the street level. I followed her down a darkened alley somewhere in Brooklyn. It's ironic that to this day I can't pinpoint my location.

The night was dark, and stars twinkled in the velvety canopy of the skies. There was a companionable feeling between us as we walked together. I never asked where she was headed or if she knew where I needed to go. I never felt the need to explain—that is, until I saw in the distance the sign "Uptown Train." That's when I remembered that I had no money to purchase a token.

Should I try to borrow my fare from her? My strict upbringing frowned upon loans from anyone, let alone a stranger. But, I reasoned, I could take her address and make sure that I repaid her.

We walked into the subway station side by side heading toward the turnstile where I could gain entrance. Just then I heard the roar of a train pulling in—my train. As I opened my mouth, she offered me the token I needed. I didn't even have to ask. Gratefully I dropped it in, stepped forward, and felt the turnstile click behind me. Heart flowing with gratitude, I quickly turned to thank her, but there was no one there.

Could she have walked away that briskly? Not really. Not in those few seconds. I thought of her slow pace and labored breathing as we'd climbed the stairs.

As I ran to catch my train, I felt excited, humbled, and awed by God's deliverance and His sense of humor—a mama with a bosom like two cantaloupes, no less. Quite likely, in my terror I might have run from a businessman in a Brooks Brothers suit.

I felt humbled because Jesus had once more been in time to attend to the minutest details of my need—and excited because I can't wait to find out who my maternal impersonator was. My angel? My Lord?

Heaven will echo with storytelling, I'm sure, because throughout eternity Jesus will patiently recount the many times—in each of our lifetimes—that He answered prayers that made no sense to anyone but Him, in His own remarkably loving way.

~~~

Cynthia Prime, a popular motivational speaker, is president of Winning Strategies. The cofounder of Parfums Llewelyn, her career includes news reporter, talk show host, author, poet, wife, and mother. She is on the board of Polly's Place, a safe house for women. Cynthia loves music and drama.

If It Weren't for Potluck, I'd Have No Luck at All

Kim Peckham

When I imagine the heavenly banquet table, I see lots of Corningware and smell Special K loaf. I guess I have a close association in my mind between gatherings of the saints and potlucks. And if we do get together for potlucks in the New Earth, you can be sure someone will show up with a casserole.

Casseroles are the culinary melting pot of the church. No matter what lies lurking in your cupboard or refrigerator at this moment, someone has made a casserole out of it. Tater tots, Nutena, leftover spaghetti, zucchini abandoned on your front porch by neighbors, Hi Ho crackers, breakfast cereal—anything seems to work if you add a can of cream of mushroom soup.

I myself use this grayish goop in my sauerkraut casserole, a dish which I have stopped bringing to potluck because the smell made people's eyes water. I began to think it might be too strong for the average taste when I noticed that it burned holes through the aluminum foil covering the dish. (I'm not kidding.)

Nobody wants to bring an unpopular dish to a potluck. Only poetry can capture the despair of a cook who must carry home a casserole dish with only a corner eaten out of it. To quote my aunt Alvaine: "It's like a slap in the face."

On the other hand, nothing matches the thrill of seeing that your casserole dish stands empty at the end of a potluck. It's as if the whole world stands up and shouts, "We love your cooking!" Suddenly, the skies seem bluer and the birds sing louder and you forget the inferiority complex you've had since the sixth grade.

Naturally, cooks strive to achieve potluck popularity. For example,

Aunt Alvaine has learned that her dishes go faster at a potluck if she adds two sticks of real butter to the recipe.

Another surefire way to make your dish more popular is to add cheese. Now I realize that cheese excites controversy among Adventists. Some will not let the substance pass their lips, earning the respect of cardiologists everywhere. But others are not so strict. They will shove aside the weak and infirm to get the last serving of a really cheesy lasagna.

Yes, cheese has mighty powers of attraction. I believe that you can bring *anything* in a casserole dish—grass clippings, fiberglass insulation, whale meat—and if you cover it with enough cheese, people will shovel it on to their paper plates.

Last week I went to a potluck that had 98 dishes (not including the dessert table) and the first one scrapped clean was a bowl of Kraft macaroni and cheese—which proves that a food item only has to be the *color* of cheese to be gobbled up without thought.

Another thing I've observed about potlucks is this. While everyone wants their dish to be well received, I've never noticed open competition between cooks. I think this is because women preside over these affairs. Things would change if men did the cooking.

If the more competitive sex took over, you'd see us skipping the sanctuary service to prepare exotic creations over a hot stove. I can imagine the lights dimming in the fellowship hall toward the end of potluck as Elder Smith makes a dramatic entry, flames shooting up from his Cherries Jubilee. Later, you hear a round of applause as Deacon Johnson proudly parades out a Baked Alaska on a sterling silver platter. And men wouldn't give away recipes either. You'd see some wheeling and dealing: "I can't let my rice pilaf recipe go that cheap, but if you throw in that old boat motor . . ."

I've seen some potlucks organized with military efficiency—everyone whose last name begins with A-C is instructed to bring a yellow vegetable, those with names D-F must bring a salad made with lime Jello, and so on.

But at most potluck dinners, participants are left to bring what the spirit dictates. Usually, things work out fine.

I think you can say the same about the church body. Some of us are far from perfect (our characters are a little cheesy, so to speak). Others wonder if they have any spiritual gifts to contribute at all. And still others feel that what they do have is not appreciated. But when the Master of the heavenly banquet table brings us together in service, we find that we have everything we need, and we need everything we have. It's like a potluck, only different. Luck has nothing to do with it.

~ ~ ~

Kim Peckham and his wife, Lori, live in West Virginia where they are conducting research to develop a potluck dish more popular than Kraft macaroni and cheese. They're not sure it can be done.

On the Road With Dirty Sally

Rhonda Reese

I tightened my sweaty palms around the steering wheel of our Nova as my husband Glenn leaned inside the car window to kiss me goodbye and set a AAA road assistance card on the dashboard.

"Have fun," he said.

"I'll try," I mumbled through a forced smile, mentally rehearsing everything my counselor had taught me about averting panic attacks. Attempting this trek—the first long-distance, overnight outing I'd tried by myself in years—meant facing my biggest fear. *Could I handle an unexpected crisis alone?*

My first panic attack

My mind raced back almost four years to the first nightmarish episode. The walls in the school where I taught seemed to turn gauzy gray. My heart raced so fast I could barely breathe. I felt an eerie floating sensation and, thankful that my students had already gone home, huddled in my classroom's closet until the attack subsided.

After that frightening afternoon I spent four weeks on sick leave. When attempts to resume teaching brought on deepening depression and more panic attacks, I was hospitalized in a psychiatric ward for five months of intense therapy. After being discharged, I continued outpatient counseling.

In the months that followed, my panic episodes gradually diminished and flickers of hope returned. But my confidence and competence were deeply shaken, and the fear of a sneak attack kept me close to home.

A few months prior to Glenn's driveway goodbye I'd surprised myself by expressing interest in attending a two-day educational conference 100 miles from home. My counselor and husband encouraged me to try it.

They helped me take short drives in preparation for the big day. Glenn even took time off from work to drive me over the entire route so I'd be familiar with all the surroundings.

A neighbor lent me her cellular phone and spent hours letting me call her from different locations around town. With enough practice, I hoped to avoid any unsettling mishaps that might send me into a panicky dither.

Dirty Sally

A week before I was to go a friend phoned. "I read an article that said riding with a companion increases traveling safety. I think you should fix up a mannequin to look like a passenger."

"A mannequin?" I asked. "Where would I get one?"

"I have one from an old school project. I'll drop her by."

"All right," I said. "Bring it over."

I named the life-sized doll Dirty Sally and dressed her to look as tough as I wanted to feel. She sported a leather jacket, blue jeans, hiking boots, a baseball cap (pulled slightly forward), big black sunglasses, and a frizzy brown wig. When I thought Dirty Sally's "motorcycle gang" outfit appeared complete, I propped her up in the passenger seat of my Nova. She almost made me smile—a rare occurrence these days.

"Listen, hon," Glenn's instruction jerked me back to the present, "call me when you get to the hotel."

If you get to the hotel, fear taunted. I chain-chewed bubble gum through the entire drive. By the time I pulled into the parking lot of the hotel—located about a mile from the conference center—a mountain of Bazooka wrappers filled Sally's lap.

"Everything went OK," I reported to Glenn from the hotel.

Before driving to the conference center, I decided to move Dirty Sally from the front seat to the trunk. "Sorry, ole gal," I apologized, smooshing her under a blanket. "I don't want people to see you and think I'm nuts."

Clearly out of my comfort zone, I was enveloped by a wispy feeling of unease during the classes. I managed to stay through the first day's evening session, but when I arrived back at the hotel, fear hung heavy in the room. I tossed and turned all night.

Oh, no!

The next morning I decided to jog around the parking lot to calm my nerves. Dropping my keys into the car trunk for safekeeping, I slammed the lid and strode off.

Twenty minutes later I returned and tried to open the trunk as usual, by twisting the black knob. Nothing happened. I rattled and twisted the knob again. Nothing. Fear rose in me like a flood.

You're an idiot, it accused. *When you slammed the trunk shut, it somehow locked with all your keys inside. You'll never get home.*

"Oh, no," I blurted. "Oh, no!" My heart pounded in my ears. I gasped for air. "Please, God, help me stay calm," I prayed. "If I have a panic attack I won't get home."

I darted into the hotel lobby. "Do you have a fingernail file?" I asked the desk clerk between gasps. "Or a crowbar? Or anything? I locked my keys in the trunk."

"Tried a locksmith?" the gentle-looking white-haired woman replied.

A locksmith. AAA. Of course. The card Glenn gave me was still on the dashboard. I ran outside, read the phone number through the windshield, zipped back inside, and dialed.

"We'll be there within an hour," a male voice promised.

As I hung up the receiver, words my counselor often said came to my muddled mind. *God will never leave you, or forsake you.*

"Never leave me, or forsake me. Never leave me, or forsake me," I chanted while circling my car. Within minutes a gray van pulled up beside me.

"I'm from AAA auto service. You the lady with the locked-up keys?" a sandy-haired driver asked.

"Yes," I answered. "How'd you get here so fast?"

"Just finished with another car up the block when I heard the call come in. I'll fix you up in a flash. No problem."

Getting my car unlocked wasn't a problem. Getting into the trunk was. The locksmith worked on the knob for at least 20 minutes, then announced, "I gotta take your back seat out and get to the trunk from there."

Remove the seat? A new wave of apprehension washed over me. *He's tearing my car apart?*

The man began unscrewing bolts. I climbed into the front seat, leaned over, and machine-gunned him with nervous questions.

"Does my husband have to know about this? Will the police come? Does this get filed on any insurance stuff? Will you bolt the seat back in when you're done? Do you think my car will be OK to drive?"

Surprise, surprise

"Hey, I think that got it," the man said, lifting the back seat up. In that instant Dirty Sally's disheveled torso rolled forward. As her head sprang out, one of her arms snapped sideways and brushed the locksmith's pant leg. "Wha—?" he yelped as Dirty Sally's wig flopped onto the floorboard.

I gasped. The man dropped the seat and shot out of my car backwards. "I'm sorry. I'm sorry. Sally's . . . she's . . . not real," I stuttered.

It took several seconds for color to return to his face. "Well, I thought I'd seen everything," he said.

"I'll . . . buy you a soda," I offered, escaping toward the drink machine. As I scampered off, a—could it be?—yes, a full-fledged giggle burst forth from deep inside me. I'd acted so nutty. And the look on the man's face when Sally rolled out! Suddenly I laughed out loud. It felt marvelous.

I returned to my car as the locksmith tightened the seat's last bolt. "Thanks so much," I said, handing him a cold drink. The man took it, cranked up his van, and drove away. It seemed that my fear was leaving with him. Locking my keys in the trunk and watching God care for me had broken something free that all the therapy in the world couldn't touch.

I made it to the morning conference on time. And that afternoon as Sally (still napping in the back seat) and I drove home, a blue locksmith van passed my car. Written on the vehicle's side in large lemon-yellow letters were the words "Jesus holds the key."

That's right, I thought with a confident smile. *Whatever future problems come my way, I'll face them with assurance that Jesus holds the key. Because He does, I need never handle any crisis alone.*

~ ~ ~

Rhonda Reese, a frequent contributor to Christian magazines, writes from Jacksonville, Florida. "Sally" hasn't gone on any more trips with her.

Love's Lullaby

Rhonda Wehler

My Internet e-mail, like my post office box, fills each day with an amazing collection of mail—from friends' notes to jokes to virus warnings. Recently there came sweet and funny baby photos accompanied by a delightful audio lullaby. I replayed the love song again and again, smiling as I pictured myself singing it to my grandbabies.

"You're my honey bunch, sugarplum, pumpy umpy umpkin. You're my sweetie pie.

You're my cuppy cake, gumdrop, snookum, baby doll. You're the apple of my eye."

Although the words weren't at all the same, the song was surprisingly similar to the love song I crooned long ago to my fuzzy-headed newborns, then later sang with gusto, patty-cakes, and tickles to my giggling toddlers.

I leaned back in my desk chair, smiling as I thought of when my children were young. Their willingness to sit on my lap in the rocker decreased in direct proportion to their growing curiosity and mobility, and all too quickly the cuddling was relegated to bedtime stall tactics.

Hold me close

But when they came down with a vicious flu it was different. While one was sleeping the other would whimper to be held. With flushed faces and abnormally hot little cheeks, they would lean on my chest and eventually relax into sleep as I sang to them and rocked. When they were sick, nothing else would do for them but snuggling with mom.

And at those times, despite demanding schedules and uncompleted tasks, nothing was more important to me than my precious children. My heart would fill to bursting with love as I comforted them through a trial that could only run its course.

As I sat at my desk reminiscing, I realized that I too have experienced the same kind of love. During times of unparalleled crisis, when only by sheer force of habit I moved from moment to numbing moment, I know I was held and protected.

When the shock of pain rendered me incapable of anything more than elementary behavior, I was, without a doubt, encompassed in my heavenly Father's embrace. I was His first priority, and His heart was filled with love and compassion for me. I leaned on Him, and He rocked and comforted me through trials that could only run their course.

It was during those traumatic times that I experientially knew the truth of His words:

"The Lord your God is with you,
   he is mighty to save.
 He will take great delight in you,
   he will quiet you with his love,
   he will rejoice over you with singing" (Zephaniah 3:17).

And I have to admit it—His love song to me sounded a lot like "You're my honey bunch, sugarplum, pumpy umpy umpkin . . ."

~ ~ ~

Rhonda Wehler, a communications manager for a community bank cooperation, is passionate about writing words that encourage. Some of her best story ideas come while she is walking. She has two adult children and four grandchildren.

My Band of Shining Angels

Jeannette Busby Johnson

The nightmare of a disintegrating marriage had brought me to the nadir of my life, my grief and despair rivaling the bleak, midwinter cold that clawed at the windows and seeped under the doors of the old farmhouse we'd moved into three months before. I moved numbly through the days and dreaded the nights, when sleep, if it came at all, was fitful and troubled.

It was on one of these nights that the ringing telephone pulled me back to unwelcome consciousness. My sister's voice, almost reverent, reached out across the many miles that separated us. She'd had a dream, she said, that had startled her awake.

Arms linked together

In the midnight stillness she'd seen my house, she told me, with snow-covered fields stretching away on every side. And suddenly, there . . . *there!* Standing shoulder to shoulder, arms linked together in an unbreakable circle that completely surrounded my house, stood a band of shining angels.

"I thought you'd like to know," she whispered, and hung up.

Returning the phone to its cradle, I turned to face the window. *Are they, God? Are they, really?*

The room was so still. So cold. Frozen. Like my heart.

A full moon's pale light fell in a fragile oblique across the floor. I pondered the sliver of moonbeam, thinking that it might shatter into a thousand crystal splinters the moment my toe touched it.

I wanted them to be there. The angels. I needed them to be there, with me and my three children, who slept across the hall.

We were so alone.

So unprotected.

So unloved.

I crept toward the window, knowing I would die if it were not so. Knowing I could not live if I did not look. Isaiah's words swirled in my head:

"For your Maker is your Husband, the Lord of hosts is His name. . . .

For the Lord has called you like a woman forsaken,

Grieved in spirit, and heartsore,

even a wife [wooed and won] in youth,

when she is [later] refused and scorned,

says your God. . . .

"For though the mountains should depart and the hills be shaken or removed,

yet My love and kindness shall not depart from you,

nor shall My covenant of peace and completeness be removed,

says the Lord, Who has compassion on you."[1]

I leaned my forehead against the glass. *Promise, God? Promise?* Then I lifted my eyes and first looked farther than I could even see, to the place where the snowy fields ended abruptly against the black night sky. Then, inch by inch, my gaze fell down the windowpane to the snow that drifted against the evergreens lining the edge of our moon-drenched yard directly below.

I saw nothing. But in a moment of overpowering awareness I *knew* they were there—my angels—shoulder to shoulder, arms linked together, faces upturned to my window.

I will not in any way fail you

nor *give you up*

nor *leave you without support.*

[I will] not,

[I will] not,

I will not in any degree leave you helpless

nor *forsake*

nor *let you down.*

Assuredly not![2]

And in these 20 years since, He has not.

Texts credited to Amplified are from *The Amplified Bible.* Copyright © 1965 by Zondervan Publishing House. Used by permission.
[1] Isaiah 54:5-10, Amplified.
[2] Hebrews 13:5, Amplified.

~ ~ ~

Jeannette Busby Johnson has three adult children and two amazingly wonderful grandchildren. Their parents had the good sense to move just down the street so "Grandma" can spoil them shamelessly. Jeannette is book acquisitions editor at the Review and Herald.

Snickers or Sneakers?

Irina Bolotnikova

W here are you going?" my husband asked as I headed toward the door.

"I need to go to the store quickly and pick up some Snickers in order to dry my coat."

"Are you sure you need *Snickers?*" he asked, not looking up from his work at the computer. I assured him that it was exactly what the label on my coat recommended.

Shrugging his shoulders, he suggested that maybe I should check with our neighbor, Helen, before rushing off to buy a box of Snickers to throw in the dryer. I knew Helen would be the right person to consult, because while we'd come from Russia to study in the United States just one year earlier, Helen had already been in the U.S. for four years!

When I got to Helen's, I told her that I was busy packing our stuff into boxes to send back to Russia and that a truck was coming the next day to pick up everything. My husband was working on labels for our belongings, and I was carefully going over my clothes before putting them into boxes. While doing this, I unexpectedly found my violet polyester winter coat. It was dirty, but there was no time to get it to the cleaners. So I carefully read the laundry directions on the label. It said that I should wash the coat in the washer and dry it with three tennis balls or a clean sneaker.

Having studied English at Andrews University for a year, I was able to carry on quite a good English conversation and could even write papers for my English classes. However, spelling was the hardest thing for me. My English teacher had told me that someday spelling would become easier and more natural, but it would take time. For now I should just carefully read the text and guess the meaning of words by the context without looking them up in the English-Russian dictionary.

At this moment it was very easy to use my teacher's rule. When I read the cleaning label I immediately pictured a favorite Russian TV commercial. It showed roasted peanuts in smooth caramel, covered with milk chocolate, and a young fellow chewing the candy bar with heavenly enjoyment. In Russian, of course, an inviting voice described this wonderful chocolate bar as "Sne-e-aker." I was sure that the word on the coat label was nothing else than this heavenly chocolate delight.

My courteous neighbor Helen told me that she had never washed coats in regular washers, so she could not say what was the best thing to use to dry them with—tennis balls or the Snickers. But she'd go to her storage room and look for tennis balls.

But I didn't want to lose any time, so I hurried to the grocery store and bought a box of a dozen Snickers bars.

Back home I put the now-clean coat into the dryer. Then I unwrapped the plastic covering off the box and threw in all 12 Snickers bars—each still covered in its individual wrapper. I closed the door of the dryer and set the timer for 40 minutes.

As I returned to where my husband was still working at the computer, he looked up and asked, "So how is your coat doing?"

I said it was well washed and now it was drying, happily enjoying the companionship of chocolate bars!

Scratching his head and turning back to the computer, he said, "Well, I have never seen my mother drying clothes like this, but it is probably a new American invention. Maybe the chocolate bar wrappers are so strong that they keep them from melting."

Finally something clicked in my mind, and I decided to go and check how my coat was doing. Opening the door of the dryer, I was really surprised to see that my Snickers bars had grown three times their original size and the wrappers looked like balloons!

I called my husband over for some counsel. He examined the balloon-big wrappers with burning fingers and exclaimed, "There is probably something wrong with the directions on your coat!"

At this moment Helen came over with her tennis balls, so I took out the candy and put the balls into the dryer, saying to myself, "No wonder so many Americans go to the dry cleaners instead of using the instructions on their clothing labels."

And several years later, when I looked in the dictionary to find this tricky word, "sneaker," I realized that the real heavenly enjoyment of a Snickers bar is not in roasted peanuts with caramel, but in strong, durable, and heat-proof wrappers!

~ ~ ~

At the time of this writing Irina Bolotnikova was the associate director of the Ellen G. White SDA Research Center at the Zaoksky Theological Seminary in Zaoksky, Russia, where she lives with her husband, Alexander.

A New Glimpse of Worship

Ann Burke

Sometimes when my husband reads to me, I fall asleep. Sometimes I interrupt. And sometimes I do listen. I was listening the other night as he read from the book of Samuel.

Since it was January, I hovered over a little heating vent while Ken sat nearby, his Christmas-slippered feet planted before him on our braided living room rug. Behind him stood the bookcase where we'd found entertainment for many a winter evening.

Ken's and my reading aloud went back to when we were newlyweds curled up with a book near a snapping fire. Later we had read to Tom, Kaye, Susi, and Danny in succession. That evening it was the two of us again.

Hannah's prayer

Hannah was the childless wife, the well-loved story went. She was also the favorite wife. From my perch near the floor heater, I listened to the account I'd known from childhood. There was Peninnah, the other wife, taunting Hannah, and Hannah running away from the family feast. Now nearing the tabernacle, there was Hannah moving her lips in prayer, in grief because she could not bear a child.

"In those evil times," Ken read from our tattered *Patriarchs and Prophets*, "such scenes of worship were rarely witnessed."* And suddenly in the familiar story I noticed something new.

"It said *worship*," I interrupted. "It said that Hannah's prayer was worship."

The rest of the reading was largely lost on me. The years rolled back, and once again it was July.

The girls were about their lives in distant places that year as apricots ripened on our backyard tree, and beside the driveway resurrection lilies waited for their time. Our son Tom had an apartment in nearby Loma Linda, California. The bunk beds he and his brother, Danny, shared as boys held only Danny on the dark early morning when we awoke to pounding on the front door and a floodlight streaming down the hallway.

Ken reached the door in record time. The conversation there was short. As I fumbled with my robe, I caught snatches of it.

"What was that about?" asked Dan, stepping from his room as soon as Ken closed the front door.

"The officer wanted to give us some information," Ken stalled.

By that time I was in the living room too.

"Was Tom in an accident?" I probed.

"Yes."

In that moment I knew.

"Was he killed?"

"Yes."

On a January evening, to the hum of my husband's voice, I pondered Hannah's prayer. And I remembered my own prayer as once in July I fell on my knees before God, on a braided rug, before dawn and wept for my firstborn son.

Why, "worship" can be simply turning to Him, I marveled. The idea touched me deeper than definition. I have to say it does so still.

---

* See the chapter entitled "The Child Samuel."

~ ~ ~

Ann Burke writes a weekly thought for a small-town newspaper from a little bedroom-made-office. It's there that she is also working on a book manuscript. Ann and her husband live in Yucaipa, California.

My New York Miracle

Mary Weiss Futcher

I walked down the street as if I were floating on air. I was a young Bible worker in New York City, and several teens with whom I'd been studying had given their lives to Christ. I was thrilled as I went to the next home.

It was after 10:00 p.m. when I left, again with wings of joy. Both parents and their teenage children in that lovely Jewish home had promised to be at church the next Sabbath.

My mind replayed the visit as I walked to the nearest subway station. I boarded the train without considering that it stopped six long blocks away from my apartment. If I'd walked another block, I could have gotten a train that would have taken me within a block of home, but I didn't realize my mistake until I stepped off the subway into the poorly lit street.

Nabbed in an alley

Bible verses were singing through my mind when a huge hand grabbed me from the back and yanked me into a dark, narrow passageway between two tall buildings. My mind raced. I felt myself go hot, then cold. I wondered wildly what the man would do to me. Would he rob me? Kill me? I knew that people had been killed for a few cents!

I had little money. My shoulder bag held my Bible, Christian literature, and a few other items. Numbness rippled through me, and I realized with terror that I couldn't make a sound.

Oh, God, save me! my heart cried.

In that instant the man dropped me as he would a sack of potatoes and ran screaming—*into the grasp of a policeman!*

When I came to my senses, I got up and went out to the dimly lit sidewalk where the policeman still held my attacker. "Are you all right?" the policeman asked me, deep concern in his voice.

"Yes, yes, I'm fine now."

The man begged to be released. He was hardly coherent and kept saying that the lightning that had struck him must have come from outer space.

I opened my bag, took out some tracts, and found myself giving them to him. After releasing the man, the police officer asked me if I'd like for him to walk me home.

Special escort

Still scared, I said yes. He talked to me of the dangers of being in such a neighborhood at that hour of the night. "God gave you a brain, and you must use it wisely," he said seriously and with such tender love that I hugged every word to myself and have always remembered his advice.

He impressed upon me the dangers of assuming that prayer would get me out of problems that I'd gotten myself into because I didn't use my head. At last we reached the lighted area of Broadway.

"Do you need to get back on duty?" I asked him.

He shook his head. "I want to see you to your apartment door."

We walked slowly, and I told him about the people I'd met with that day, of the teens who'd given their lives to Jesus, of the family who'd promised to come to church. He listened carefully, interested and happy at the way God had blessed.

My steps slowed as I reached my apartment. The doorman opened the outer door and I nodded to him, then turned to thank the policeman. He wasn't there.

Puzzled, I turned to the doorman. "Did you see where the police officer went?"

The man frowned. "I didn't see anyone, miss. You came to the door alone."

In my apartment I fell down on my knees and thanked God for His wonderful deliverance. The next morning I phoned the police stations in my precinct and in the area I'd been attacked, asking the name of the officer who had been on street duty. At both stations I was told that only patrol cars had been in the area.

With great awe, I thanked God again for sending His angel to save me and walk me home.

~ ~ ~

Mary Weiss Futcher sold Christian magazines for many years, and deeply loved her Lord. She passed away in 1997. This story is reprinted from *Guide* magazine.

O Keys, Where Art Thou?

Kim Peckham

One of the benefits of family life is that there are always people around who will respond to your plea "Has anyone seen my keys?" Or, to be more accurate, there is the hope that someone will respond.

In reality, your family members are unable to give your problem the slightest attention because of pressing concerns of their own, such as fingernail hygiene or looking through *Sports Illustrated* to see the latest photographs of sweaty men.

I have lost many things, including socks, retainers, and the entire body of learning from my sophomore year of college. But this thing with my keys is starting to wear on my usually sweet disposition.

It's like being forced to play a game of hide-and-seek with myself. My hands drop the keys someplace; my brain goes off and counts to 100; then it tries to find the keys again.

Now, I can hear someone saying, "Why don't you put your keys in the same place every time?"

Well, maybe I *am* putting them in the same place. I just can't remember where that place is.

The good thing about losing your keys is that it can reinvigorate your prayer life. I'm almost surprised that the Lord's Prayer doesn't make a place between "Give us our daily bread" and "Forgive us debts" for a little something about "Return to us our keys before we're late for work."

Speaking of the heartbreak of personal loss, my wife recently had an incident involving her toothbrush. I wasn't thinking clearly one morning, and I accidentally picked up the wrong toothbrush—*her* toothbrush. Well, let's just say she never used it again. I'm thinking: *We're married! It's not like she's sharing a toothbrush with a viral research monkey.*

My wife also gets upset when she loses receipts. That's because without a receipt she can't return items to the store, and she eventually returns *everything*. From her perspective, a department store serves the same function as a bank. You give them both money. Then they both give you a piece of paper that you use to get the money back. Only the department store is superior because it also gives you a stylish new blouse.

But perhaps I am drifting from my topic, which is basically as follows: People lose things. This is the chief reason that God did not give us removable body parts.

"Hey, Mom. Have you seen my ear?"

"Check the pool filter, honey."

While we are troubled by losing things, finding things is a joy. In fact, some people make a hobby out of finding the things that their fellow human beings have lost. Recently I read an Internet posting by a man with a metal detector who was enthusing about a particularly good day at the beach.

"We found four pennies," he recalls with satisfaction, "and two hotel keys in separate spots, and a large stainless-steel spoon made in Norway."

You get the feeling that if he ever found a quarter, the excitement would give him an aneurysm.

We're happy to gain, and sad to lose. Every bad feeling I can think of is about loss. We're grieving loss or fearing loss or just plain angry about loss. When we are losers, we are weepers.

Jesus proposes to change this. He encourages us to let go of things so that they will no longer have a hold on us.

I recently attended a funeral, and even in the midst of the most painful loss, the agony was blunted by the hope of the resurrection. There is the sense that most of what we are afraid to lose isn't very important, and if it is important, it will be restored to us someday with compounded interest.

That is a key to peace of mind that no one can afford to lose.

~ ~ ~

Kim Peckham, director of periodical advertising for the Review and

Herald, has lost many things in recent years, including some hair around his temples. His parents, he adds, have lost their investment in his piano lessons. He and his wife and son live in Falling Waters, West Virginia.

He's Always There

Dan Roberts, as told to Corrine Vanderwerff

I paused by the kitchen window as Bob, my pilot husband, jumped Gary, our giggly 15-month-old, to the ground, then turned to catch 3-year-old Eric. An old cistern at the corner of our mission house made a perfect platform for the boys to jump into Bob's arms. I sighed. It was good to see him and the boys playing, but . . .

Well, it had been a difficult year. Just today Bob was back after another two weeks of flying in other parts of the country; I seldom saw my only close friends—they lived an hour's drive away. I had nothing in common with the villagers.

"Don't go!" we'd been cautioned when we were offered a transfer to Zaire. "Here you can get out easily. You have medical and shopping facilities. But *there!*"

We didn't have do it, but flying is Bob's life. As young adults we'd dedicated ourselves to serving the Lord, and soon after our marriage, when Bob was asked to be a missionary pilot, we'd gladly gone to Africa.

"Lord," I'd finally prayed, "if You want us to go to Zaire, make me willing."

Gary was 2 weeks old when we moved.

Our new home included a comfortable house, neat brick hangar, good airstrip, and lots and lots of outdoors for the boys. Hills to our east swept up into the volcanoes of Africa's continental divide; to the west, hills rolled down into the vast forests of the Zaire basin.

But I wasn't happy. I was a trained nurse and a pianist, and used to being involved. "I can see no useful purpose in my being here," I murmured aloud.

Look! The silent voice made me turn toward the window. I saw Bob leaning over the cistern's edge, pulling something from the water.

"Gary!"

I ran. Bob could safely crash-land an airplane, but he wouldn't have the least idea of what to do for a drowning baby. Grabbing Gary, I flung him over my knees.

Get the water out!

My thoughts raced. This wasn't just some medical emergency. This was my son! Fear numbed my mind, but my nurse's hands moved methodically. Water gulped out.

Breathe!

My hands continued their rhythmic motion, willing tiny lungs to respond. The body remained limp, motionless. Moments spun toward eternity, then I felt a convulsive shudder. Gary's chest heaved. He struggled . . . gasped for air . . . was breathing . . . was sitting up. A healthy rose returned to his cheeks, and he smiled.

We tried to reconstruct what had happened. Eric jumped, and Bob caught him. When he looked up, Gary was gone. Bob thought he'd slid down and come to me, but something prompted him toward the cistern.

Workmen had been repairing the downspout, and its protective guard was missing. Bob groped in the murky water, and Gary's shoe bobbed up. He grabbed at it and was pulling Gary out when I'd had the compulsion to look out the window.

"What ifs?" rushed in. What if Bob had come to the house first? What if I hadn't looked? But all was well, and we thanked God.

A few days later Bob flew out with the mission plane again. Rain settled in, and so did my resentments. God had given me the willingness to come; He'd shown His care in Gary's rescue. But He had put us where I could see no practical use for my nursing skills and musical talents.

Then Gary developed a chest cold. The next day, exactly two weeks after his accident, his temperature soared. He developed a raw wheeze and couldn't keep anything down. I did what I could with simple household antibiotics, but as the afternoon wore on, his fever climbed higher.

Ironically, Bob's duties included emergency medical airlifting. We maintain daily radio contact when he's flying, but even if he had been near enough to come, heavy clouds had socked in our valley. Landing was impossible.

A mission hospital lay two and a half hours to the north by road. I could handle the winding mountain terrain in our four-wheel-drive pickup. But alone—with a 3-year-old and a dangerously sick baby? On dirt roads in the rain, at night, when I wasn't sure of the way?

Gary's body burned hotter.

"God, help me to know what to do," I prayed. And then I knew I needed to go for help.

The school is between our airstrip and the hospital. Bundling up Gary, I hustled Eric into the truck. Despite the rain, we made it to the school in good time. "Evelyn," I called, bursting into a friend's house. "Gary's sick. What should I do?"

One look at him and she said, "Get him to the hospital."

It was quickly decided that her husband, Elton, would drive. Bonnie, their neighbor, would come to help with the children. I cradled Gary close as the tires slugged along the rain-mushed road. We arrived at midnight.

"Bronchial pneumonia and paratyphoid," the doctor said, ordering immediate medications. Bonnie and I stayed with Gary. Elton and Eric slept in the next room. Bonnie stretched out on the bed and dozed off. I pulled a chair close to Gary's cot. The flickering candle, our only light, cast grotesque shadows on the wall. Then suddenly Gary began to writhe, chattering in weak syllables, pointing at things I could not see.

I tried to reach through his hallucinations to soothe him, but his arms flailed feebly against mine. "God," I cried out soundlessly. "Help him! Please!"

Gary continued to twist and turn.

As I sat helpless to do anything more, I began to feel a oneness with the mothers beyond our airstrip. I'd seen so many sad faces after measles or dysentery or malnutrition had snatched little ones from their arms. And I had seen the rows of little raw earth mounds in village cemeteries.

Unnecessary, I thought as I looked down at my own fever-ridden son. *If they just had the proper medical treatment.*

The hours dragged by. Finally Gary's breathing seemed to relax. The fever slackened. I continued to sit, to watch, to pray. Gary quieted, then slept. At daybreak Bonnie roused. "Let me watch him for a while," she offered. "You need some rest."

Gratefully I let her take my chair.

Instead of lying down, though, I slipped out into the morning. Above me the mountains towered against the sunrise, their majestic peaks lifting toward the heavens. "God," I whispered, keenly aware of His mighty power around me. "I . . ."

Suddenly my pent-up emotions became a torrent of words—not just about Gary, but about my discontentment, my frustration, my loneliness. I opened up honestly, turning all my feelings over to God. Suddenly a peace like I'd never known settled around me. Assurance came. Gary would be all right.

The doctor let us take him home later that morning, loading me down with medications and instructions. Within a few days Gary was his sunny self again. For me, though, change had begun.

I'd been having a Sabbath school for just Eric and Gary. Now I invited the local children to join us. Some came. They loved the singing and Bible stories, and brought friends. That was the beginning.

Trust developed, and their mothers started bringing children to me for treatment, then vaccinations. Then I was holding regular vaccination programs, nutrition classes, well-baby clinics, and workshops for children's Sabbath school teachers. One event built on another. We built a clinic. It continued to grow until now it's a full-scale health center with maternity, treatment, and teaching rooms just down the road from the airstrip.

God had given me the willingness to come to Zaire, but not until the near loss of our own little boy did I begin to realize that He could use my talents there. On that long-ago morning I had no idea of what the future held. I simply became aware of God's presence and realized that no matter where we are, He is always there.

~ ~ ~

Corrine Vanderwerff, a professional author and missionary, now lives in Alberta, Canada. She enjoys their good biking trails, extra time with her grandsons, and easy contact with good friends. She is a frequent speaker at women's retreats.

Filling Eyes and Ears With Beauty

Alicia Patterson

It was a hot summer night in Plano, Texas, 1970. I was 5 years old, and I was bored. The days had gotten longer; it was still light outside, but I'd been put to bed.

I turned to my side and waited for sleep to come. I looked up at the ceiling and waited for sleep to come. I turned so that my legs were high up on the wall and waited for sleep to come.

It didn't.

I started kicking my feet—slowly, slowly—on the wall. *Thump. Thump. Thump.* It was strangely comforting. *Thump. Thump. Thump.* I was surprised my mom hadn't come yet. ("Lisa, quit kicking the wall," she would say.) *Thump. Thump. Thump.* I decided to keep kicking until she came.

Minutes passed. I lost track of time. When she finally came to my room I was still kicking but had forgotten why. Lost in the rhythmic thumping, I was surprised when the light from the hallway shone in my now-dark room. Even more surprising was the way Mom gently addressed me. "Are you not tired?" she asked.

"No," I said.

"Do you want to come watch TV with me?"

Stunned, I just followed her down the hall, skinny legs in a little nylon nightgown.

She was watching a ballet. I don't remember which, only that it was beautiful. I loved the music and the graceful dancing ballerinas. At its close I walked sleepily down the hall and climbed gratefully into bed, my mind's eye filled with whirling and leaping, its ear with beautiful music.

Sweet sound

A rainy night in Vienna, Virginia, 1998. He awoke about 8:30 p.m., whimpering. He is 20 months old. The whimpering increased to a cry, and even after I picked him up it crescendoed. I couldn't fully awaken him from his nightmarish sleep and carried him, still thrashing and crying, into the living room, where my husband lowered the lights. We sat and rocked, and looked out the window at the red and white car lights reflecting in the wet pavement. I talked to him in a low voice while he sipped carefully on his bottle of water.

Ten minutes passed. Gable was still awake and a little restless. We moved to the couch, and I wrapped him in his special blanket. Geoff slipped in a video of Irish folkdance, and our son watched the rhythmic dancing, hearing the mournful sound of the Irish instruments and the crystal-clear voices of the singers. As he watched and listened his nightmare tenseness fell away, and he relaxed in my arms. His eyes and ears filled with beauty, he began to drift off. I carried him to his crib, where at once he fell into a deep sleep.

My turn

Now my thoughts turn to You, Father. I thank You for a loving family and for the beautiful boys You have given me. I thank You too for Geoff. And I thank You that sometimes when I'm bored and kicking naughtily or too caught up in the nightmarish reality of this world to be comforted by reason, You pick me up and carry me in Your arms.

Through Your Word, through music, through the thoughtfulness of friends, I gain glimpses of a better place. I see a place where harmony and rejoicing and light are the norm. And with my mind's eyes and ears filled with beauty, my soul calms. My stride takes on the cadences of a heavenly rhythm. And I resolve once more to rest in You.

~ ~ ~

Alicia Patterson writes from Columbia, Maryland, where she is getting a refresher course in "How to Do Laundry and Other Household Chores While Holding a Nursing Baby." Alicia is engaged in the awesome task of rearing three little boys to be godly men.

A Gap in Your Agapé

Heide Ford

Frustrations flare as the subtle glow in the east penetrates the mist-enshrouded Lake of Galilee. The seven have worked the nets all night with not a fish to show for it. Nothing seems to be working out lately. Fishing has been their life, but somehow they've lost their touch. Jesus, whom they followed and loved, was crucified, instead of crowned. And though He's risen, it's not quite the same.

What does one do after they've invested themselves fully in one cause, in one person, and then suddenly He's gone? What's next? And where is Jesus? He said they'd meet in Galilee.

As always Jesus is near, though veiled by mist. And as the disciples act on His word, they haul in a catch of fish beyond their imaginings (see John 21).

Hungry, tired, and wet the disciples huddle around a hot coal fire while Jesus serves breakfast. Awe settles on them for they're again in the presence of the God with whom their lives have been indelibly interwoven.

As smoke curls up from the hot coals, the pungent odor draws Peter's mind back to another coal fire on a cool morning in the high priest's courtyard several weeks before. His cursing denials have haunted him ever since. Jesus has forgiven him, but can he forgive himself? He's been in the inner circle; can he be trusted again?

"Simon, son of John."

The question

Peter is jarred out of his reverie hearing his full name called. It's Jesus talking, but He's not using the nickname He'd given him—Peter. (It means rock, but he surely hasn't been acting like one lately.)

"Simon, son of John, do you *agapaō* Me? Do you love Me with a divine love that is solid as a rock? Do you love Me with a love controlled by principle, not feeling?"

"Yes, Lord, You know I *phileō* You. You know I love You as a dear friend—spontaneously, wildly even."

"But Simon, son of John, do you *agapaō* Me? Do you love Me at all costs, even to the sacrifice of yourself?"

"Yes, Lord, You know I *phileō* You. You know I'm deeply attached to You."

"Simon, son of John, do you *phileō* Me? Are you truly fond of Me, or is your love superficial?"

"Lord, with all the time we've spent together You know that we're good friends and how much I care for You. You know I *phileō* You."

Three denials, now three confessions of loyalty.

Though Peter could only admit to endearing friendship instead of the higher, purer, self-sacrificing love, Jesus knew that he would grow into *agapé*. He accepted Peter where he was at and called him to serve.

Are you attached to Jesus? Are you fond of Him? Do you love Him wildly and spontaneously? Jesus is glad for *phileō* love, yet He also wants you to grow into *agapé* love. A love that won't change with your moods or circumstances. A love that when you're tired of trials, tired of sacrificing, tired of trying and you want it your way, that you'll still say, "not my will, but Yours be done." A divine love that can grow only as you walk and talk, work and play, with the Divine One.

Yet be assured that when your fondness flounders or your wild emotions wilt and there's a gap in your *agapé* and even your *phileō* flops, Jesus' love is everlasting. He accepts you and forgives you. Then He calls you to serve.

~ ~ ~

Heide Ford, associate editor of *Women of Spirit*, holds a master's degree in counseling and has a special place in her heart for dolphins (she's swum with dolphins) and whales. She and her husband, Zell, live in Maryland.

Over 40 and Pregnant

Crystal Earnhardt

I stared at the little pink dot, my legs feeling weak and shaky, my thoughts frozen. I heard laughing and foot stomping close to me, but I couldn't focus on it until a pair of strong hands encircled my waist and swung me in the air.

"You're pregnant! Really pregnant! I'm going to be a daddy again!"

What was wrong with this man? Didn't he know that he was 45 and I was—well, over 40? "Oh, honey, this is so exciting!"

He gently placed me on the bed and reached for the telephone. "Who should we call first?"

My mouth opened, but nothing came out. My lips felt numb, as if I'd just visited the dentist.

"Oh, honey. You're too happy to talk, aren't you?"

The room suddenly became quiet. So quiet that I could hear the clock ticking on the living room mantle. "You *are* happy, aren't you?"

I tried to analyze my emotions. Happy? Well, I was happy a week ago when our youngest daughter graduated from five years of college with a degree in psychology and married the man of her dreams the very next day. My husband and I celebrated. We bought a bottle of fake champagne and went out to eat. No more school bills! We could afford to eat at the Olive Garden again. Why, we might even get that trip to Hawaii that we'd dreamed about for so long.

And I was happy when our oldest daughter phoned to say that her little boy was walking quite nicely and that she loved working in the hospital's OB Department, taking care of the moms and babies. I'd felt smug with satisfaction. Both kids had their degrees, had good jobs and a family.

Now I could relax and enjoy some of the things I'd never had time to do.

I wanted to think about that emotion some more. *Happy could mean . . .*

Suddenly my stomach rumbled, and I made a dive for the toilet. Who could think happy thoughts with morning sickness?

My own mom was more optimistic. Now in her 80s and energetic as ever, she doubled over laughing when I broke the news to her.

"You think this is funny?"

"Lighten up," she said. "You'll go through menopause with no problems."

"Why?"

"Because you'll be too busy to notice," she told me as she howled with laughter.

Waiting . . .

The next seven months dragged by. I felt like a school kid waiting for Christmas. An extremely fat school kid. I developed all of the symptoms of pregnancy. *All* of them. One night I stretched in bed, and a searing pain stabbed my leg. I reached down and felt a knot. I couldn't put any weight on it.

"Leg spasms are quite normal in pregnant women," my daughter—the mom/baby nurse—informed me the next day. Didn't you have them when you were pregnant with me?"

"No."

"Well, it's common. No need to worry. Another thing, Mom—you'd better eat plenty of fiber. You know pregnant women have trouble with—'"

"Yes, dear, I know all about that."

"Mom."

"What?"

"Do you remember that babies can't have popcorn until they're 2 years old? And no honey until they're 1? It . . ."

So this is what role reversal feels like.

My husband took this pregnancy very seriously. "I think I'd better ask for a transfer back into pastoring," he mentioned over dinner one night.

"Why?" I held the spaghetti-laden fork in midair.

"My job with the church requires too much traveling. I'm not dragging a baby around the world, and I don't feel comfortable leaving you. I've been wanting to settle down anyway."

"But we'd have to sell the house and move."

"I've been praying about this," he replied, "and I know this is what God wants me to do."

I was too tired to argue. Months later I found myself sitting among hundreds of unpacked boxes in a new house. At least it was closer to my daughter. In fact, she picked out my OB doctor and hospital. I couldn't seem to make decisions anymore, so I just went with the flow.

I was sitting on the couch watching TV when my water broke. My calm, knowledgeable husband suddenly went to pieces. He hustled me out to the van. He ran back in to find the video camera. Minutes later he rushed to the front door. "Where's the camera?" he yelled. I went back in the house to help him find it.

We headed back out to the van, he with the camera and me with a packed suitcase. "Oh, let me take that," he offered. But when we reached the van I looked around for the case, and it was nowhere to be seen.

"Where's my case?"

"What case?"

"The one you just took from me with the baby's going-home outfit."

Another trip back inside.

Finally we reached the hospital. Our daughter was waiting at the door with a wheelchair and three other nurses—her best friends and most trusted coworkers. It had been a slow night, so I got all the attention. They chatted cheerfully among themselves as they did all the gruesome procedures expectant moms must endure at the hands of nurses.

Hours passed. Long hours.

The contractions intensified, and I was taken to the birthing room.

All sorts of people filed in and out. Most of them glanced my way, pity written all over their faces. My son-in-law looked too happy. He was enjoying every minute.

"What's Me-maw doing?" my 2-year-old grandson asked.

By now the pain came sharp and searing. I ordered all the family out but my nurse/daughter and my husband. My son-in-law looked crushed.

"This isn't a picnic," I snapped, glaring at him.

Get out!

"But I'm good at coaching," he insisted. "You should have seen me when Robby was born."

Clenching my teeth, I pointed to the door.

For hours I ate crushed ice and sweated through the most excruciating pain known to women. At this point I was feeling quite stupid for refusing the epidural.

I heard the doctor mumbling and the nurse yelling at me to push. I'd already been pushing for an eternity.

"Breathe!" My husband was feeling quite useless and couldn't think of anything else to say. He repeated the same word like a broken record. "Breathe. Breathe!"

"What do you think I'm doing!" I snapped back.

I looked up from my sea of pain. A whole circle of faces stared at me, each one making a different demand. "Push." "Breathe." "Push." "Breathe." The pain reached phenomenal heights. Why in the world did I ever decide to do this all natural?

"Get the forceps," I heard the doctor whisper to the nurse.

"Absolutely not!" I was getting mad now. "You are not using forceps on my baby!" I held my breath so hard that my cheeks were full of air. I must have looked like a chipmunk hoarding nuts. Then I gave it all I had, practically coming off the table in one gigantic effort to rid my body of this pain.

Everyone cheered. Then suddenly the doctor flopped this bloody baby on my stomach. My daughter dropped her camera and sprang into action, ready to rush the baby to a little cubicle in the corner where she suctioned her mouth and cleaned her. But for one brief moment I make eye contact with this little creature. It's as though I've known her for some time but can't wait to know her more. My husband smiles and pats me and tells me what a beautiful baby we have.

"She's worth all the agony and pain," he remarks.

I glance toward the corner where my oldest daughter is busily working over my newborn daughter. "She looks just like Mom!" I hear her exclaim.

"Honey"—he seems a little alarmed by my silence—"she is worth all the agony and pain, isn't she?"

"What pain?" I answer him.

~ ~ ~

Besides being a mom again, Crystal Earnhardt is a pastor's wife and freelance writer. She enjoys quilting and gardening and her ever-growing, precious little daughter Carrie Ann. Crystal and her family live in South Carolina.

"Got Any Milk in There?"

Crystal Earnhardt

When Carrie Ann arrived, my heart melted into a little puddle. This was my third and last child. I was over 40 and had two grown, married daughters—the older with a 3-year-old son and the younger, a newlywed.

I well knew the fleetingness of childhood. Looking back, it seemed that one day I held my girls in my arms and the next day I carted them off to school. The hours in between were almost a blur. I couldn't remember their first kisses on my face or what day they took their first steps. Maybe I was too busy, or too young. But I made up my mind that things would be different with Carrie. I would savor this child like homemade soup. And so I recorded her first laugh, her first words, and her first teetering steps. I memorized her smile and the print of her chubby hands. While most mothers couldn't wait to put their infant to bed, I couldn't wait for Carrie Ann to wake up.

You can imagine how much I loved the intimacy and warmth of breastfeeding. I never wanted to wean her. One year passed in a heartbeat. My pediatrician suggested that I could gradually omit one feeding at a time. "But it's up to you," he hastened to add when my face turned white and I almost tipped backward off the chair. "Some mothers nurse longer."

At her 2-year checkup he told me that I should seriously give weaning some thought, but he quickly changed subjects when Carrie frowned at him. Then came the jokes. My son-in-law loved to describe what he thought would happen on Carrie's first day of school. "The teacher will announce lunch period, and she'll look around for you!"

Even my husband began to worry. Up until this time he'd been very supportive. But now Carrie was voicing *her* opinion. "I'll stop nursing when I'm this many," she said, holding up five chubby fingers.

I ignored their jokes and unsolicited advice until Annabel became involved. Annabel is my 87-year-old neighbor. She's pretty lonely and often accompanies me to the grocery store just to get out of the house. Annabel doesn't hear well, so I'd explained to Carrie that she had to talk real loud if she wanted Annabel to hear her.

On this fateful day the plan was for Annabel to push Carrie around in a grocery cart while I shopped with a separate cart. Without the distraction of a toddler, I could get done quickly.

All went well, and we were soon in the checkout line. I began putting the groceries on the counter. In the cart behind me, Carrie was tired and hungry. I glanced back to check on her and realized that she must have noticed Annabel's breasts for the first time. They were at eye level for a wee person strapped in a grocery cart! And those two lumps in her blouse could mean only one thing. Lunch!

Carrie reached out and touched one, then the other. "Annabel," she asked, "you got any milk in there?"

For once I was glad Annabel had a hearing problem.

But Carrie must have remembered my earlier advice. "Annabel!" she called a little louder. "You got any milk in there?"

I could hear a snicker from three grocery carts back. I began emptying my cart with the speed of a jackrabbit. Annabel didn't seem to notice.

Undaunted, Carrie punched each breast one at a time, and with her little Southern accent she drawled out the words as loudly as she could. "ANN-A-BEL! YOU GOT ANY MILK IN THERE?"

By now everybody within 50 feet was laughing. I stared straight ahead, acting as if I didn't know anybody. Much to her credit, my precious neighbor lowered her head and pretended not to hear a word.

Annabel didn't say much on the way home, and I had no intention of bringing up the subject. But two hours later my phone rang. I picked it up and heard her raspy laugh on the other end. "Crystal," she asked, "did you hear what Carrie asked me in the checkout line?"

I did what I always do when I'm uncertain what to do. I played dumb. "H'mmm. I heard her asking for a banana once."

"She asked me for more than that," Annabel giggled. She then proceeded to tell me the whole story. She could barely talk for laughing so hard. I was glad it gave her something to laugh about.

Two hours later the phone rang. It was Annabel again. I knew it before she said a word. All I could hear was her hee-hawing on the other end. "Crystal, I just can't quit thinking about it." She laughed some more. But then her voice grew serious. "It's your business what you do, but when children can reason as well as Carrie Ann can, it's about time to stop."

I knew it was time too. My heart felt as heavy as a full dishpan. I knew this was goodbye to babyhood. Letting go is so hard. Now I understood God's longing when He cried over rebellious Israel "How can I give you up?"

Carrie ignored me when I explained that she was a big girl now and didn't need Mommy's milk anymore at bedtime. (We had omitted all feedings except the bedtime one.) She cried herself to sleep that night. I cried after she went to sleep.

The second night she begged, "Just a *little* milk, Mommy!"

The third night she went into a Peter Pan yell: "I don't want to grow up!"

When I explained that the milk had dried up, she burst into tears. "Make it come back, Mommy." (Now I know why they recommend weaning before kids can talk.) A three-year daily habit is hard to break, and it wasn't easy for her. Every night for two weeks her pitiful pleas broke my heart. "Please Mommy, just one side."

That was three months ago. And now as I watch my 3-year-old manipulating the mouse on the computer, I realize that it hasn't been easy . . . for me.

As for Annabel? She was glad to hear that the "Dairy Queen" finally closed.

~ ~ ~

Crystal Earnhardt and her husband, John, live in Fair Play, South Carolina, where Carrie Ann is keeping them young. They have two adult daughters as well.

Daddy's Girl

Wendy Wilkinson

I've always been Daddy's little girl.

My friends say I act just like my father, sound like him, even look like him. Take away his gray hair and beard, and I have to agree they're right. I'm a duplicate of my dad. I even think the way he does.

Dad has always been my hero. As a preschooler I spent entire days following my mother around the house, asking, "When will Daddy be home?"

The answer was always the same—not soon enough for me!

We loved going on adventures. One such adventure was making a 10-mile canoe trip down the Potomac River with a group from church. It was my first time to go canoeing with my dad, and my 8-year-old enthusiasm couldn't have been matched by anyone present. I was definitely one happy camper.

The day was warm and wonderful. It didn't take me long to get the feel of paddling, and soon Dad and I were ahead of everyone else. I had a paddle in my hands and water behind and ahead and splashing all around. What more could a kid want!

Unfortunately 10 miles was a lot farther than I thought, and after a couple of miles my energy was zapped out. The paddle that had made me feel so powerful was making blisters on my hands. Even the water didn't seem enticing. My arm muscles burned, and my back screamed. I began wondering why Dad had dragged me out here.

Would we ever see home again, or would I just die paddling? It couldn't get any worse than this.

Immediately Dad sensed my mood. "Wendy," he said, "we're going to make it, and ahead of everyone else. You know why?"

"Why?" I grumbled.

"Because we're *Wilkinsons!*"

It may not make any sense to you, but the determined and steadfast way he said our name gave me all the will I needed. We were in this together, and I was gong to make it. Dad would be with me all the way. No way was I giving up. You know why? Because I'm a Wil-KIN-son!

The rest of the trip we continued the chant, two pumped up voices echoing over the water.

"We're going to make it, and ahead of everyone else! Why? Because we're Wilkinsons!"

By the time we reached our destination there wasn't a bird, animal, or person along the river that could possibly have missed that fact.

In the boat of life we all have a heavenly Father, who, like my dad, knows we can get tired of our life and despair of ever reaching our final destination. The distance is far too much for us on our own. We're frustrated. We want nothing more than to give up and bail out.

But He's in the boat with us, encouraging us, telling us that we're going to make it. And why? Because we're God's kids. We're daughters of God.

He's our hero. We pattern our lives after His.

Don't you just love being your Daddy's girl?

~ ~ ~

Wendy Wilkinson was a high school junior when she wrote this story. She loves the outdoors, photography, drawing, York peppermint patties, and guys.

A Cat Tale

To Anne Jamison, as told to Darlenejoan McKibbin

Three weeks old, so starved that most of his hair had fallen out, a tiny kitten was left on our front lawn for us to find, rescue, and love. His body was soft and pink, like a baby pig's, so we named him Piggy.

He grew to be enormous and porky and, I admit it, the favorite of our four cats.

I was at work the day the people came to clean the rugs.

The unsuspecting worker put his machine down in a corner near a sleeping Piggy, then turned it on. Piggy leaped straight up. Yowling, he streaked through the house to the kitchen, and found the back door open and the screen unlatched.

Out he went, right in front of the man who was mowing the lawn. Another yowl, and Piggy raced down the street and out of sight.

When I came home that night, my husband, Don, told me what had happened. I took a blanket for warmth and sat in a chair by the back door, crying and calling Piggy all night.

It was raining the next day, but I went up and down the block knocking on doors, asking neighbors to check their garages, calling in vain for Piggy.

I made up a flyer describing him, and a friend and I took it door-to-door in a four-block radius from home. It was still raining and we got wet, but that didn't matter. Daily I went to the pound and checked the cages. No Piggy.

Don reminded me I had three other cats. He didn't seem to understand that three cats safe at home did not alleviate the worry I had for the one stray declawed cat lost in a world it didn't understand. Piggy depended on me. I had to find him.

130

After a week Don asked one of my friends if she thought it would help me to rescue a stray cat from the pound to replace Piggy. She wisely advised him, "Don't suggest it." She knew that a new cat, even a needy foundling, wouldn't end my worry about the one that was lost.

Still praying

I prayed, "God, You know where Piggy is. You can bring him back to me or help me find him. Please help me. Please."

I received a lot of calls in answer to my posters, and I went to each person calling to see the cat they'd found, but none of them was Piggy.

Another week ended. It had been more than 15 days since Piggy was scared away. I received a phone call around 10:00 p.m., and a man said, "I think I've found your cat."

He lived four unit blocks away and had been hearing cat howls for a couple weeks, but thought they were just a wild cat's calls.

However, this night the howls came from under his daughter's window and were accompanied by a strange bumping sound. The child wouldn't go to sleep until he investigated. And looking behind a warped crawl space restrainer, he found a cat drowning in a cesspool.

I ran over in the rain and looked into the crawl space. It was Piggy! I pulled his emaciated body out of the filthy water, hugged him to my chest to protect him with my rain slicker, thanked the man, and ran home.

I washed him, cradled him in a soft towel, and comforted him beside me the entire night.

The next day I called the friends who had understood and who had marched door-to-door with me in the rain looking for Piggy.

"He's dying," they said.

We found an emergency veterinarian nearby. X-rays and tests were taken. The tests showed that Piggy had a good heart and lungs, but that he was malnourished and dehydrated. He'd lived on his own fat while he was trapped, and would have died of starvation otherwise; but the vets feared that his liver had been damaged. They didn't know if they could save him or not.

Then followed three weeks of daily pilgrimages to the Emergency Pet Hospital.

Piggy couldn't eat, so he was force-fed. They had him on IVs to combat his dehydration. He lost most of his hair and soon was as naked as he was the day we found him.

He still had hair on the end of his tail, but it was slimy wet. "Gangrene," the vet said. "His tail will have to come off."

"Save him," I ordered.

I decided Piggy could stay at home at night when the vet finally coaxed him to eat from her finger. Don and I could feed him in four-hour shifts until he was well.

I called the vets the other day to tell them Piggy was well. Then I stopped by the pound to tell the volunteer there that they could take down his poster. When I told her I had found him, the woman, whom I'd never met before, was overjoyed. "Oh, how wonderful! Is he all right? How is he psychologically?"

I was touched that she would care, and that she understood Piggy had suffered great stress, loneliness, fear, isolation, depression, and feeling of abandonment while lost—something most people didn't realize.

I told them I loved Piggy so much that I cried every day and every night; that even the cats I still had couldn't console me. I looked high and low every day, and I wouldn't give up looking until my cat was found.

If I could show so much love and concern for a cat, how much more does Christ Himself search for us, refuse to be consoled, and continue to search until we are safely within the fold of His loving arms?

Separated from God, the lost soul suffers distress, loneliness, fear, isolation, and feelings of abandonment just as Piggy did. God knows and understands this.

Christ ministers to the wounds of the prodigal. He feeds the hungry thirsty soul, nurturing until that person is strong and whole, as well as saved.

No one is written off because of the wounds their lifestyle may have inflicted on their soul. Once found, once we are safe in God's arms, He will restore what is needed, as well as provide a lasting home of safety and love.

My cat taught me this truth about God.

~ ~ ~

JoAnne Jamison founded Psalm Ministries to feed God's sheep who are in prison pastures through her own musical talents and a Bible correspondence course she developed especially for them. She and her husband share a passion for grandparenting.

The Day I Met Michael Jordan

Ginny Allen

was at the airport waiting for someone to arrive when I heard an excited murmur around me: "Look! There's the Chicago Bulls!"

I looked across to the next gate and saw all these super-tall guys. "My son really loves basketball," I said casually to the people next to me. "He'd have liked to be here right now."

"You should go get some autographs for him," one said.

So not being shy, I trotted over and looked way, way up, and believe me, since I'm barely five feet tall, it truly was way up. "Rumor has it that you guys are the Chicago Bulls," I said.

"Rumor has it right," one of the tall guys answered back.

I told them about my son—though I didn't mention that he was in college—and said that he'd love to have their autographs. So they all started signing the scrap of paper I'd found in my purse. Then one of them pointed to a *really* tall guy coming over to the group. "That's the guy whose autograph you need," he said.

As "that guy" came up to us, I told him, "These guys said I need *your* autograph."

He laughed and added his signature to my little scrap of paper. We chatted a bit; then I thanked them all and wandered back over to my gate.

Michael Jordan's autograph

Then a man who'd been watching the whole thing came over. "Did you really get their autographs?" he asked.

"Sure did!"

He pointed at the last one who'd signed. "Did you get *his* autograph?"

"Sure did!"

Then with amazement in his voice he queried, "Lady, do you know who that man is?"

"Sure don't!"

Now, I want you to know that today I would recognize Michael Jordan, but that was his first year or so as a player, when he was really just starting to be *the* name in basketball. So I knew his name but not his face.

The man responded emphatically, "Lady, that's Michael Jordan!"

Then he pulled out his billfold, started counting money, and said, "Lady, I'll give you $500 cash—right now, on the spot—for that autograph."

But since there are some things that money can't buy, and I knew my son would love having it, I said, "No, my son will want this."

However, as I look back on that day, I have often wished that I had taken the money.

You see, I called my son that night and he was so excited he could hardly wait to come home. He said, "Mom, I'll be home in two weeks to get it!"

But somehow between the time of the phone call and the anticipated arrival, I lost Michael Jordan's autograph!

And by the way, that little scrap of paper is worth much more today. His autograph goes for thousands today and is usually given only to auction off for charities. At least that's what I read somewhere, and I like to believe it since it helps my story along.

I'd been so excited over getting that autograph for my son because I knew he'd like it. My intentions were so good, but the autograph was lost in spite of my good intentions. And it was lost, I have to admit, because of my carelessness. Once in a while, all these many years later, my son will still say with a tone of wonder in his voice, "I can't believe my mom had Michael Jordan's autograph and LOST it!"

Careless or busy?

In the end, though, an autograph is just an autograph. In the great scope of life those things really don't matter too much. But can you imagine losing the one thing that matters most in life because of either carelessness or busy-ness? I can think of no greater tragedy than losing the one thing that really matters to me—my relationship with Jesus. To lose it because of my carelessness or my busy-ness is almost unspeakable.

The Bible says, "For what will it profit them to gain the whole world and forfeit their life?" (Mark 8:36, NRSV).

Daily spending time with Jesus is my way of keeping our relationship strong and healthy. The more time I spend with Him, the better I know Him. The better I know Him, the more I love Him. The more I love Him the more I trust Him.

Trust is a must-have for any relationship. It cements the love foundation of the relationship. Trust is what keeps me loving Him when I'm not sure where He is leading me. Or why.

There have been lots of whys in my life and quite a number of wheres.

I love stories of answered prayers, and I've had more than my share of those. But I find in my life that the whys and the wheres keep my hand most firmly in His. The whys and the wheres are the testing of my trust— a trust based on the love God and I have for each other.

For me, that is what prayer is all about. Knowing Him. Loving Him. Trusting Him.

It won't change my life if I never find Michael Jordan's autograph. What has changed my life immensely and eternally is the decision daily to do whatever it takes to spend time with Jesus. To know Him, to love Him, and to trust Him.

In the great scope of my life, that's what matters most.

~ ~ ~

A nurse and health educator, Ginny Allen is a frequent speaker at retreats and prayer conferences where she shares personal stories and her message "Serving God With Joy."

Thank You, Daddy

Philip Crouch

Some simple decisions have profound effects.

The decision to have a baby is one of these, a choice made without counting the cost. Indeed, how could one be able to count it?

And so, that decision of love is born—a living, lifelong responsibility. And life is never the same.

My daughter Nadia was born with acute renal failure. Her kidneys were not developed, and underdeveloped, respectively. Her chances of making it out of the neonatal intensive-care unit were slim at best. Yet here we were, five years and numerous medical milestones later, contemplating a kidney transplant.

Another choice, another far-reaching, little-understood decision.

"You're a good match, Mr. Crouch."

"Your daughter really needs to get this kidney soon."

"We've scheduled your 'living donor' surgery for four weeks from today."

"Everything is ready, Mr. Crouch."

"Just sign these release papers."

May cause permanent injury or death . . . or death . . . or death.

Real love

It's times like this, when you're so afraid, when the unknown of the future forces you to your knees, that you suddenly catch the smallest glimpse of what real love is all about. Love that compels one against all reason to offer something so much a part of themselves to another who is in need.

At 6:00 a.m., Tuesday, April 10, 2001, Nadia and I groggily made our way to the surgical waiting area at Johns Hopkins. At 6:30, after getting the IV placed and donning the surgical stockings and "privacy" gown, I sat with my family, waiting for the first surgery of my life.

My first hospital stay.

The first time we'd have two of our family members under the knife at the same time.

Then—unexpectedly, like a surprise gift, or the joy of sudden good news—we looked into the face of Jason, our pastor and friend. He'd left his home a great while before dawn to be sure he could pray with us before we went into the operating room. In that one selfless act God provided the comfort and assurance that we needed. I can honestly say that I went into surgery without fear or regret, and with the unmistakable peace that only God can provide.

Then it was over. I remember well the first painful trip I took to visit Nadia in her intensive-care recovery room. I arrived in my wheelchair to find a small antiseptic enclosure so jammed with medical technology that I had a hard time getting into the room.

I looked down at my little girl, lying still, hooked up to all those machines. Her face pale. Her weak body loosely wrapped in a child-sized gown. Her tired eyes met mine, and her tears began to flow, but a soft smile formed on the edges of her lips. In a moment that will be forever framed amid the cobwebs of fading memories, she raised her arms to my face and whispered, "Thank you, Daddy. Thank you for my new kidney."

Living donor gives all

And suddenly it made me think of my Father–my heavenly Father. The Father that I have not always loved as my daughter has loved me. The Father that, at times, I've turned my back on, have willfully wandered away from. And I wonder anew at *His* love.

How can it be that He would take my place? Not a kidney, not a bone-marrow transplant, not a piece of a liver, or a blood transfusion—none of these were options for Him. I needed a new heart, and you just don't get a new heart from a living donor.

No, my Father had to give everything.

His scars still speak of the lengths to which He was willing to go. A love so strong that He would lay down His life for His child. And all at once I see His face as He leans over my weary form. His tears fall onto the pillow beside me, and in my mind's eye I reach out to His nail-pierced hands and whisper, "Thank You, Daddy. Thank You for my new heart."

~ ~ ~

Philip Crouch lives in Maryland with his best friend and wife of 14 years, Jeannette. They have two daughters, Natasha and Nadia. He enjoys spending time with his family, the outdoors, and with woodworking.

A Mother's Prayers

Betty Rayl

I never met Grace, yet her life of faith and prayer has had a profound influence on mine. When she died at 53 from complications following surgery, she was at peace with God. But it was not always so.

Grace was 20 when she married "Blackie," a brawny young blacksmith. His nickname matched his profession, dark hair, swarthy complexion, and sullen moods.

The dowry Grace brought to the marriage was a bent for hard work, a frugal nature, and a 9-month-old baby girl. Blackie gave tiny Dorothea his name, but he never forgot she wasn't his child.

Most brides cherish dreams of happy-ever-after, but the reality facing Grace left no time for dreams. The vegetables she coaxed from the rocky soil fed her family year around, fresh in summer, canned in winter. Milk, butter, and cheese came from cows she milked by hand. Three meals every day were prepared over the wood cookstove that scorched the cook as it cooked the food.

More hardship than happiness, more privation than plenty. The one constant supply was babies. Diphtheria claimed the lives of three, and a tiny girl was stillborn. She was baby number 14. Grace was 37.

Blackie's sullen moods turned violent. Grace packed up her two youngest children and moved to town. She found work keeping house for a widower. In the 1930s most women stayed married no matter what. Grace divorced Blackie, remarried, and birthed a towheaded baby boy, number 15.

Gossips had a field day. Her grown children refused to speak to her. The better life she longed for was still beyond her reach. Then Grace met

Jesus, and joy came pouring in and filled every corner of her being.

Her new husband thought the evangelist was interesting. Toddler Johnny drew roads in the sawdust at their feet. But in those meetings Grace found meaning and focus for her life. As the years passed, her faith grew stronger as her body grew weaker—and she learned to pray.

Little towheaded Johnny was growing up surrounded by bad influences. Even his dad had no real interest in spiritual things. He was a kind man and a good father, but he hardly knew God. He used tobacco and had an occasional beer. Grace didn't want her son following in his father's footsteps—so she prayed.

~ ~ ~

The junior Bible lessons from the Voice of Prophecy were discolored by age. I smiled at 9-year-old Johnny's childish scrawl as he answered the questions.

On the back page the handwriting changed. I read, *Please pray for my boy, that he will grow up to be a Christian.* Signed, *His mother.* Grace was praying for Johnny every way she could.

My tears splashed on the paper, because I knew that not many months later Grace would go to the hospital for surgery and never return home. How could God answer her prayer when she was laid to rest? I don't know how, but He did!

Grace prayed for her boy the first 10 years of his life. I have prayed for him and with him these past 40-plus years. Johnny is my husband, and Grace is the mother-in-law I never knew.

Her prayers continued to guide and protect Johnny through his teen years and kept him close to God. I'm sure she would be happy to know how he helped me make a Christian home for our family. Her prayers were answered.

I'm eager to see the reunion when Grace meets her little Johnny, now grown tall. We'll sit together at Jesus' feet while He explains the mysteries of love, forgiveness, and the miracle of a mother's prayers.

Doesn't that sound like heaven?

~ ~ ~

Betty Rayl wrote this when she was the women's ministries director for the North Pacific Union. She and her husband, John, have always lived on a farm and raise cattle, sheep, hay, and grain. They have four adult children and 12 grandchildren.

Taught by a Wave

Sally Streib

I stumbled along the narrow path etching the cliffs above Laguna's green waters. So often I'd felt heartaches ease after a walk high above that tossing sea. Somehow by the ocean God had been able to smooth my troubled thinking with His gentle hand. But now thoughts of my mother's death still screamed through my mind.

As I watched her die day after day, grief swelled inside me like a giant wave. I'd vowed to be strong, but I felt suffocated by sorrow. I wanted to cry for help, but the words caught in my throat. I needed to grasp the comforting hands of friends, but I was a frozen statue. Most of all, I ached to admit my helplessness and pour my heart out to God, but I couldn't speak.

Suddenly I scrambled down the bank and plunged into the sea. Surfacing, I gasped to see a rising wall of water not five feet away. It mounted up, high, high over my head.

Dive quick! Dive quick! my instincts screamed. I hesitated, gulped air, and plunged into the wave. But I dived too shallow and too late. Sea water poured into my lungs, burned my eyes, and tore at my hair. Then the wave spit me out.

I stared at the shore a long ways away. I desperately needed help, but no one noticed. Boys tossed food to squawking seagulls. Little girls patted the sides of wet sand castles. Women had their faces hidden behind magazines. No one realized I was too weak to fight the water. No one knew I could actually drown.

I heard another locomotive of water gathering behind me and willed myself to move, but my legs crumpled. The wave grabbed me and tossed me around and around like a wet towel in a dryer. It flipped me over, tore all the air from my lungs, and tossed me toward shore.

"Need some help?" a voice called. I looked up and saw a lifeguard holding a red life raft under one arm.

Did I need help! *Yes, yes, yes,* I wanted to scream. But for one foolish moment I hesitated. I saw the cluster of people on the shore. They'd watched the bronzed lifeguard jump from his tower, grab a life raft, and dash into the water. They'd craned their necks and peered through shaded eyes to see him swim to me—the thrashing, limp victim.

Suddenly I wanted to be strong. I was a scuba diver. I'd dived in half the seas around the world and never felt fear. Surely I didn't need help now, so close to shore.

But the sea roared again and my determination buckled. "Yes, please help," I called, reaching toward my saviour. The lifeguard grabbed me in his arms and quickly drew me to land.

The crowd clapped. They clapped because the lifeguard had done his duty well. But they also clapped because I'd had sense enough to know my weakness and my need of his strength.

Soon I huddled within the cocoon of a warm blanket. I'd come to realize my utter helplessness. I'd felt the saving arms of the lifeguard and dry sand beneath my feet.

In that moment of helplessness, I learned anew a valuable lesson. Sometimes we need to accept our weakness and grow strong in the comfort of God and friends.

With God's help, I'd be able to do it.

~ ~ ~

Sally Streib draws on her love of nature and the Word to conduct weeks of spiritual emphasis in church schools, to teach seminars at women's retreats, and to guide teachers in using lessons from nature in their classrooms. She lives in Palm Harbor, Florida.

The Adoption

Nancy Rockey

Ann moved into the hilltop parsonage with her newly graduated pastor-husband, two toddler daughters, and an eclectic group of furniture. Across the street 40 cows grazed in a green, hilly pasture. On one side a heavily treed lot blocked vision of a house set back from the dead-end road. On the other a backyard swing promised the possibility of children at that house.

For nearly five years Ann's little girls played with the two little girls next door. Ann and her neighbor, Melody, became good friends, visiting almost daily over the fence or in the backyard as the children played. When Harry and Ann opened a chapel for the local community, Melody and her family attended. Together the families ate pancakes on the porch and vegeburgers at the backyard picnic table. Theirs was a solid friendship.

Eventually Ann's family was transferred to another district, and gradually the two families lost touch. Now and then Ann thought of their earlier days, their hilltop home, and their friends next door.

Several pastorates and 20 years had passed when Ann's phone rang one late-summer morning. A familiar voice said boldly, "Ann, is this you? I've made 17 phone calls to find you, and finally the lost is found! This is you, Ann, isn't it?"

"Yes! Is this Melody, my hilltop neighbor?"

"Yeah, you wanderer, it's me. How did you know it was me?"

"Your voice. It hasn't changed in, well, 20 years. And your bubbly personality hasn't changed either, Melody. Why in the world would you be looking for me?"

"Well, before that, how in the world are you? How's the 'big guy,' and how are the girls?" And so for the next few minutes and across 2,000 miles, the two old friends played catch-up, chatting about husbands and children and life.

"All right, girl," Ann said at last. "Why did you search for me? It must be something important."

For a brief moment the line was silent, then Ann heard a deep sigh. Melody's changed and broken voice tearfully told the story.

Melody told of her youngest daughter's desperation to have a baby. She shared how Susie and her husband had purchased and were living in the old parsonage on the hill, right next door to Melody. They'd planned to have several children, so had invested in the big old home, fixed it up, then saved their money. They were ready for a family, but nothing happened. Months and many tests later, it was determined that one of the couple was sterile.

"They've looked into adoption, Ann, but the cost is in the thousands, and it takes years! They don't want to wait until they're old to have a child." Melody paused, and Ann could feel that she was trying to remain calm. "They're desperate," Melody continued, "and somehow I thought of you. Couldn't get you out of my mind. So, do you have any ideas? Can you find them a baby? Will you help us?"

Ann was speechless for a few seconds, then began to sputter. "Melody, I'm dumbfounded! First of all, it blows my mind that you actually found me, and second, that you would have such a request. I hardly know what to say. I'm a counselor, but not an adoption counselor. I just have never had a baby plunked in my lap, Mel, even though I wish I could tell you otherwise."

"But you have so many connections, Ann! Will you just try to find us a baby? If anyone can, you can. Please, Ann, please!"

Such confidence and expectations. Ann sent a *Help me, Lord* heavenward, and responded with more confidence than she felt.

"I'll tell you what, Melody. I'll surely pray about this, and I'll inquire where I can. Please assure your Susie of our love and concern for her and her husband. Tell her too that Harry and I will take this to the Lord regularly. He will provide the wisdom. And if any opportunity presents itself, I'll call you. OK?"

"That's all I can ask for, Ann. We'll trust God on this end for your wisdom."

The conversation, lasting nearly an hour, left Ann awestruck. As she busied herself with household duties, her mind wandered to memories of the past. She continued to pray as she dusted and vacuumed. "Twenty years and 2,000 miles have separated us, and this old friend calls me. What are You asking, Lord? You show me what to do, and I'll do it," she prayed as the day ended.

Nearly eight weeks passed. The information Ann gathered was not hopeful. The statistics regarding affordable adoptions were discouraging, since most unwed mothers keep their babies. Ann hadn't given up, but the future didn't offer much hope.

Then one autumn evening a former church member and good friend came to visit. She appeared unusually tense and preoccupied, so Ann came right to the point.

"You seem to be really upset, Joy. What's the burden you're carrying?"

At that Joy burst into tears. "My daughter is pregnant!" she blurted out. "Unmarried and pregnant. What will we do?"

Ann sat beside her friend, and they cried together.

"I've been there, Joy. I know what you are thinking. I hurt with you. This was my story just a few years ago. Your tears are quite appropriate. Are you feeling disappointed in her, or maybe in yourself? Are you angry, embarrassed, or just plain devastated?"

Together they wept and shared their feelings. Ann comforted Joy until her friend's tears subsided.

"Well, first of all, Joy, let's get her to the doctor. We need to find out if she really is pregnant, if that home pregnancy test was done accurately. And we need to know the due date."

"But she wants to have an abortion! I can't stand the thought of it, but she insists that's what she wants. That's what her boyfriend wants her to do too," Joy cried.

"Right now I'm sure that she feels abortion is an easy way out of her problem, but a doctor's visit and hearing the baby's heartbeat may change all that. Let's arrange an appointment right away. I'll talk to her and help her to understand the importance of seeing a doctor."

Several days later Joy's daughter lay on the examination table. Her pregnancy was confirmed and a due date established. As the doctor used the Doppler to amplify the baby's heartbeat, tears streamed down the young mother's cheeks.

"There will be no abortion! This is a live baby!" she exclaimed. "But what'll we do, Mom? How can we manage? I'm so scared."

"We'll talk to Ann. She'll have some thoughts," Joy assured her.

Later Ann and the teenage mother-to-be sat quietly in Ann's office. Ann knew she must deal gently with this fragile girl, creating an atmosphere of love and acceptance. Hours passed as the girl shared her feelings and vented her anger at all of the varied results of a poor choice. Slowly she progressed toward decision-making.

"It wouldn't be best for me to keep the baby," she told Ann. "I would love the sweetness of a new baby, but I'm afraid that soon I'd resent the hours of demands on my time, and then I'd resent the baby. My folks would end up raising it while I went to school. I'd lose my teenage years. I'd hate my folks for parenting my baby, and I'm afraid the baby would be confused about who's really its mother and where its father is. My boyfriend broke up with me shortly after he found out I was pregnant, so the baby would have no dad."

"Do you see any other options?" Ann asked.

"Somehow we have to find a home for the baby. But I want to keep in contact with the baby and its family. I would want to have pictures, and I would want the baby to have a picture of me and my family. Maybe I could even see it once in a while. I don't think I could stand never to see the baby, or to have it think that I wanted nothing to do with it. Do you think that's possible?" she asked Ann as she wiped tears from her eyes.

"Why, yes, it is possible. It's called an identified adoption, and works well when there are cooperative folk on both sides."

"Can you help me to find a home? I don't want this baby to go to any of my family. That would just cause confusion for everybody, and I'm afraid people would end up lying about who's who. Know what I mean? I don't want the baby to live anywhere around here, because I'd go crazy looking at every baby! Can you find a couple somewhere, away from around here? Can you find a good home, Ann?"

Slowly the young woman's fears subsided as Ann shared the story of the long-distance phone call she'd received several months earlier. Ann described the house where the baby could live. She shared her memories of the baby's possible grandparents—her old friends, who would live next door. She created as many word pictures as she could, and promised to look up old pictures she might have of the house and the family.

"Well, Ann, call them and tell them you have a baby for them! That's what I'll do. I'll give the baby to them. If you know them, and if you think they'd be good parents and the baby can grow up where your kids grew up, then that's what I want to do!" The young mother's resolve and determination were strong. She left Ann's office confident that the right decision had been made.

Ann waited several weeks to call her friend. She talked to the teenage mother numerous times, making certain she was clear in her mind about the decision. She didn't want to raise any false hopes for the family longing for a baby of their own. At last Ann felt it was safe to call, and when Melody heard Ann's voice on the phone, she screamed with joy.

"Are you calling me with some hopeful news? Do you know how Susie and Tom can get a baby? I knew you were the one to call!"

Scores of phone calls followed—with the birth mother and adoptive mother, between grandparents on both sides, and between Ann and her faraway friends. Letters and pictures were exchanged.

The months passed. The teenage mother asked Ann to be near her when the baby arrived. Ann will never forget it. Susie waited outside the delivery room, pacing the floor, hearing every birthing cry, praying for the woman giving birth. When the baby girl arrived, she was wrapped and placed in her young mother's arms.

The girl held the baby close, touching her gently, whispering, loving her. "I love you so very much. It's hard for me, but because I love you, I have chosen to give you to a whole and healthy mommy and daddy. I was able to give you birth, but I cannot be a mother." Gentle kisses punctuated her words. Grandma Joy, Ann, and even the doctor wept as they heard the mother's words and felt a little of the sacrifice she was making.

Then Susie and Tom were called and the newborn baby was given from mother to mother. The joy and sadness of the moment overwhelmed them all.

~ ~ ~

I am Ann, and today as I write this, Tom and Susie are one year into the joy of parenting their gift from God. The toddler is a constant reminder of a young woman's difficult sacrifice and the miraculous inter-vention of a loving heavenly Father.

I wonder what God must feel when His once-hopeless children find joy in His Son. And what must Jesus feel, as Creator and Redeemer, as He presents a new child of God to its heavenly Dad? I can only imagine.

Isn't it incredible that a loving heavenly Father would look with com-passion upon the pain of a childless couple and the sorrow of an unwed teen, and would allow me, a pastor's wife who knew them both, the thrill of bringing them together to benefit the child? Twenty years and 2,000 miles are nothing at all to Him. And oh, the glory of being used by God.

~ ~ ~

Nancy Rockey, a counseling psychologist and nurse, is assistant direc-tor of Family Life Skills with Faith for Today. She and her husband, Ron, travel extensively, giving seminars. She enjoys needlework and music.

Join My Judging Ministry

Kim Peckham

I am willing to judge people. This is a service I provide without charge. People can come to me, and in just a few minutes I can let them know where they fall short of my standards and the steps they can take to improve themselves.

I don't even need to meet a person face to face to judge them. For example, I can judge you as you read this column. No offense, but wouldn't your time be better used by cleaning up the kitchen?

So you may be asking me, "Why are you willing to take time out of your busy schedule to provide this service for the public?"

Why? Because I care. I want to do my part to make the world a better place. And if I can do that by pointing out your flaws . . . well, I'm just glad I can give something back to the community.

For example, you may be driving too slow. I'm happy to bring that fact to your attention with a helpful toot of the horn. Or let's say I disagree with your method of disciplining children. I'm happy to point out the areas where you are being too lax. People say they find my point of view particularly "fresh" because it has not been biased by the actual experience of having children of my own.

Now, you may be wondering, *How can I get involved in this ministry?* I'll tell you, it's easier than you think. We each have been given, in a larger or lesser degree, the gift of discernment when it comes to other people's defects.

I, for example, can tell when people use the word "hopefully" incorrectly in a sentence. Because I've been given this special gift, I feel obligated to point out the mistake when I overhear it in a conversation at a restaurant or in a store. You might be surprised by the shocking lack of appreciation that some people show when I offer them assistance in their grammar. (I didn't think people were supposed to hit you if you wore glasses.)

You may think, *How will I find time for a judging ministry with my busy schedule?* Yes, you'll have to give up a portion of the time you spend minding your own business. But this ministry comes with rich rewards.

Judging has an invigorating effect on your self-esteem. You can almost get to the place where you forget about your own shortcomings if you take time to focus on the faults of others. It's a good, good feeling when you realize that, hey, at least you're not as bad as other people.

For example, you possess a great deal of integrity compared to that city councilman who took bribes from the garbage company. Of course, some of the vendors you order from at the office *do* send you some mighty nice gifts. But in that case, it's just the spirit of Christmas.

I hope you will consider taking up a judging ministry of your own. Right now someone you know is doing something wrong. Let them know it hasn't escaped your attention.

By the way, step over here a little closer. Is that a speck in your eye?

~ ~ ~

Kim Peckham, the director of periodical advertising for the Review and Herald Publishing Association, tends to judge people who are terrorists, who market tobacco, and who have call waiting.

Love's First Claim

Eithne Amos-Nuñez

Leaving Canada to spend a couple years in Paris seemed a good idea after the divorce and the sale of our home. There I was, like someone out of a B movie, a woman in her 40s seeking meaning for her life. But I was serious about myself and registered for French classes, lining up with about 50 young students of various races and languages. I saw no one else from Canada and certainly no one my age.

The French course included visits to museums and historical landmarks. On one of these outings I met Shawki, an Egyptian gentleman in his mid-40s who was also divorced. Together we toured the Paris of little bistros, parks, fountains, and sidewalk cafés. Soon we were able to converse easily in French, the language of poets and romance.

When Shawki proposed marriage, I felt jarred out of my escapade and into a world of reality. We were opposites. He was a Muslim whose culture at its most extreme wrapped up women in veils, encouraged public prayer five times a day, and amputated the hands of thieves. By contrast, I was an atheist and a free-spirited extrovert to whom the word "submission" conjured up an image of abject slavery.

However, my growing attachment to Shawki made me reason that he was different. He was an internationalist with a Ph.D., working for his government in Paris. We could compromise. We could be happy.

Hearing a voice

One Sunday afternoon I lay on the sofa reading a French novel for class. The pale December sun filtering through the tall window cast a comfortably warm glow. Letting the book drop to the floor, once again I pondered marriage to Shawki. In that instant a voice, clear and melodious, echoed through the stillness of the room. "Get up and go home and set your house in order," it said.

It seems strange to me now that I never questioned whose voice it was or where it came from. Jumping to my feet, I began to search for my passport. When I told Shawki my plans, his typically Oriental reaction was reassuring. "Our time will come," he said, always seeing God's will in everything. But I felt that my life had taken a new turn with that compelling voice that called me home.

Back home I found a job and tried to settle down to the humdrum routine. Winter turned into spring, and memories of Paris surfaced as I eagerly read Shawki's regular letters. Then one day I received something in my mailbox that intrigued me. "The Arab-Israeli Conflict," it read, describing a series of lectures. I decided to attend.

Upon arrival, I saw a table stacked with Bibles, and my atheistic vehemence was aroused. "What has all this to do with the Arab-Israeli conflict?" I demanded of the hostess.

"The speaker is going to discuss the Middle East crisis from the perspective of Bible prophecy," she said gently. "You do want to check it out for yourself, don't you?"

And so I found myself with a Bible in my hand, being ushered toward the auditorium. "Oh, well," I said to myself, "since I'm here, I might find it entertaining."

A large screen stood behind the speaker. As he spoke, the texts he used flashed on the screen. His presentation centered on the divine authority of the book I held unopened in my lap, and I shrugged my shoulders at each point he made. But suddenly he touched a nerve. "God reasons with man," he said.

"Reasons? God reasons?" I muttered to myself. Remembering my childhood, I wanted to stand up and shout "You're a liar!"

"You must never ask questions," my teachers had told me. "You must have blind obedience." And thus I saw God as an unreasonable dictator. A God who suffered no objections to His rule, not even to satisfy the curious mind of a child.

Come, let us reason

Then a Bible verse flashed on the screen, and its simple message shook the very foundations of my atheistic beliefs.

"'Come now, and let us reason together,' says the Lord,
  'Though your sins are like scarlet, they shall be as white as snow;
  Though they are red like crimson, they shall be as wool'"

(Isa. 1:18, NKJV).*

Like a laser, those words penetrated the darkness of my mind. Could it be that God exists and *He* desires to reason with *me?* I tried to grasp the implications of such an idea as I rapidly reread the words.

"Though your sins are like scarlet . . ." *Yes, yes, I know they are,* I thought, recalling my history of sin and rebellion.

"They shall be as white as snow." *How?* I thought frantically. *How?*

"Though they are red like crimson . . ." *Yes, I know they are.*

"They shall be as wool." *But how can red be white, and how can sins once committed be made to vanish?*

An impossible glimmer of hope suggested something unimaginably precious for me in these words. The awesome possibility that God could exist confronted me in those words, words of invitation and promise.

I could reason with Him right now, I thought. Without moving my lips, I said, "God, if You have been there all along, why didn't You swat me like a fly all those years when I denied You and hated Your name?"

As clearly as if He had spoken aloud, I heard His voice, full of love: "How could I slay you? I have died for you."

Then as though I were present at Calvary, I saw Jesus hanging on the cross and dying for my sins. As my mind tried to grasp this, a flood of tears coursed down my cheeks, splashing onto my hands and wetting the cover of the Bible I still held in my lap. The knot of unbelief that had gripped my heart for so many years snapped, and a strange new joy surged up inside me.

"He loves me?" I asked myself incredulously.

Yes, with a better love than I ever knew. I knew then that He had always loved me and that He had followed me through my wayward life, patiently awaiting a moment when I might respond to His love. Amazing discovery! All I had ever done was worthy of death, but He offered me the gift of life.

"What do you say, Eithne? Will you accept My love?"

In solemn awareness that God waited for my reply, I said, "Oh, yes, dear God. Yes! I want You to be my God, and I want to be Your child."

Emerging into the sunlight that evening, I felt myself aglow with love toward everyone and everything. A song of praise broke from my lips.

A letter from Paris awaited me that evening, but I left it aside unopened. *How insignificant is human love,* I thought, *compared to the love of God, which now fills my whole being.*

My life took a complete U-turn after that extraordinary encounter with God. I became a self-supporting missionary in Ireland, and in due course the Lord chose a husband for me after His own heart. Jaime and I both agree that God has first claim on our lives and that wherever He sends us, there we will go, confident in His promise "Lo, I am with you always, even to the end of the age" (Matt. 28:20, NKJV).

~ ~ ~

Eithne Amos-Nuñez and her husband, Jamie, spent two years in Peru teaching English and computers at Inca Union University. Eithne enjoys gardening, decorating, and homemaking. She is currently working on a book on prayer.

Baby Steps to God

June Allen Beckett

Eight o'clock Monday morning. I eased into my chair in our workshop and reached for a tool to continue a wood sculpture I'd begun the week before. Bob, my husband, was still in the house, but I could see his project laid out on the workbench.

The phone rang—not unusual, since much of our business was conducted by telephone.

"Good morning. Beckett Originals," I said.

"Mom?" A male voice sounded so strained I didn't recognize it.

"This is June Beckett speaking. Who is calling?"

"This is Mike. Here in Nome, Alaska. Mom, they're all gone. Barb and the kids . . . " Mike's choking voice trailed off, and another man came on the line.

"Mrs. Beckett, this is a friend of Mike's. Barbara and the three children died when their home burned last night. He wanted to be the one to tell you, but it's too hard for him." He gave me a few more details, and I arranged to call back as soon as we notified other family members.

Trying to cope

Our loss was devastating. Each of the family did the appropriate things, but we walked in our own valley of the shadow, getting through each day by putting our hands in God's. However, after a while I realized that attending church each weekend left me emotionally demoralized. I'd go there needing comfort and spiritual sustenance. And though our church family let us know how much they cared, I'd come home drained.

Realizing that something was very wrong, I began to pay close attention to what was happening to me. As I analyzed my time at church and prayer meeting, it seemed that I was hearing constant preoccupation with the time of trouble, that time of chaos before Christ returns.

All around me people were saying, "I want to study more so I'll be ready for the time of trouble." And "Pray for me so I'll be ready." I heard sermons echoing the theme, and adult Bible study classes veered off into discussions of how to be ready for this difficult time near the end of the world. Some of my neighbors invested in extra freezers, grew bigger gardens, and talked of how our country community was "an ideal place" to be when the trouble came.

Wasn't anybody wanting to be ready for Jesus to come?

Bob and I talked this out. We discussed Elijah of old and how God had provided food and a place for him to stay during a famine and "time of trouble" in his country. We realized that now, more than ever, it was important that we be ready for Christ's return. We wanted to see Barbara again. We wanted to gather Becky and Debbie and Stephen in our arms and carry them to meet Jesus!

"God, help me"

My grief simmered. I begged the Lord to direct me, and He answered swiftly. Into my mind came the thought *Go to the children, to their Sabbath school! Their songs are of heaven. Their teachers are telling them what you need.*

I phoned the leader of our children's class and asked if I could come and sit and listen. "Please don't give me anything official to do—I can't handle it," I said. "Just let me share what you give the children. OK?"

I walked into the roomful of children. Little ones smiled at me. A child climbed on my lap, and chubby arms hugged me. We sang "Everything's all right in my Father's house." We repeated finger plays, with big, bright pictures of Jesus and His angels coming to earth. Watching the children's faces, recognizing their simple faith, brought healing and gradual resolution of my inner feelings.

I became the resident grandma. With no specific responsibilities, I could share the children's joyful emotions. I soaked up the simple message of Christ's gift of salvation. Toddlers carried flannel cutouts to the board to complete the cloud of angels coming with Jesus. My heart walked with each child as they went forward.

Slowly I handled my grief. The loving trust of children whom I drew onto my lap gave me part of the relief, but a lot of help came from the simplicity of the message. At the end of a year my ability to function as one of the adult congregation seemed to come back quite naturally.

Bob and I believe wholeheartedly that there will be "a time of trouble" (Daniel 12:1, KJV). But the children's simple faith gave me the message that I needed—walk every day with Jesus.

We'll see you soon, Barbara and Becky and Debbie and Stephen. Jesus is coming again!

~ ~ ~

June Allen Beckett writes from Tennessee, where she has turned her hobby of creating and collecting dolls into a means of giving new life to worn dolls, which are then donated to a thrift shop. Proceeds are used to help local people in need.

Thumbprint of an Angel

Betty Pierson

My heels dug into the blacktop. Fingers tried to grasp the pavement. But slowly, relentlessly, I was being bumped and scrubbed along the blacktop pavement. I can't breathe. *I can't breathe. Will my life end like this?* my mind cried. "Mama," I yelled. "Help me!"

Mom and I were returning from a good doctor's appointment, and our hearts were light. She was hungry, so I pulled the car into the parking lot of Taco Bell. It had just started to sprinkle as I walked around the car and opened the passenger door.

As Mother moved her foot to step out, the car began to roll backward. I had no time to think; I could only react. Frantic, I pressed my weight in front of the open door, trying to keep it from rolling into the traffic. Of course, that was impossible. Then I tried to jump clear, but it was too late.

I felt I was being crushed. But the pressure did not stop, and I did not die.

The weight of my body finally slowed the car down. It had rolled up the side of my hip, then rolled back, and stopped. I was lying on my back beneath the open passenger door. From the waist down I lay underneath the car. My right hip was jammed against the back of the right front tire. I wanted to move but was afraid the car would roll into traffic if I crawled out. I needn't have worried. The right front tire was parked firmly on my skirt.

A trucker stopped his rig right in traffic and ran over to help. I asked him to pull my car forward so I could get out from under it. Finally the car was moved, and I was helped to my feet.

I checked my legs and wrists and decided nothing was broken. I didn't even have a bump on my head. So I got into the car and sat quietly for a few moments to collect myself. Then, surging with adrenaline, I said, "Well, Mom, let's get you back to the nursing home."

Off to the ER

I was wet and chilled when I arrived home and told Don, "I nearly killed myself today!" When I explained, he couldn't believe I'd driven Mom to the nursing home and myself home afterward. I wanted nothing more than a hot bath, but Don wouldn't hear of it.

So off we went to the emergency room. Several X-rays later I was told that I was all right. I felt that I had a cracked rib or two, though the report said "No definite breaks." My wrist was badly swollen—it *looked* broken—but the X-ray showed no break. I had several cuts on my legs and large bruises on my back and hips and above my knee.

A few days later Don and I visited the place of the accident. When he saw where my handbag had dropped when I fell and then where the car had stopped, he was shocked. "Betty, you were dragged 30 feet. You shouldn't be alive!"

This experience, though painful, brought a renewed sense of thankfulness to God for His tender watch care. Sometimes when we think of the battle between Christ and Satan for our souls, we don't think of the care God gives to our bodies. I feel that the devil had planned to take my life, but God must have told him, "Well, you can bump her a little, but you can't have her."

I've heard tragic stories of others who had lost their lives in similar experiences. How very merciful God was to me. Most of my injuries have healed, though I still have a large indentation on my right wrist and a lump on my right thigh.

As I related the experience to a coworker, he said, "Betty, this dent in the top of your wrist looks like the thumbprint of an angel where he held you firmly to keep you from greater harm."

We all face trials and troubles, but no matter what lies ahead I'll always praise God for His love and care in this frightful experience. And I thank Him for leaving His angel's thumbprint on my wrist to remind me that I am loved.

~ ~ ~

Betty Pierson, recently retired to Florida, loves reading, gardening, and nurturing people. She and her husband, Don, have three daughters and five grandchildren.

Sara's Hands

Penny Estes Wheeler

Sara sank onto her bed and looked at her hands in disgust. Rough peeling skin, ragged fingernails, and she had neither the time nor the energy to care. She didn't have time for anything these days, what with trying to combine a career with homemaking and, she thought, doing a poor job of both. Then her eyes caught the snapshot of her grandmother she'd taped to her dresser mirror, and she blinked back tears.

Toiling hands

Grandma's hands had washed diapers and dirty faces, plucked chickens, and doctored chigger bites. They'd quilted with tiny stitches, crocheted lace, and hemmed napkins and skirts. They'd beaten countless egg whites and cake batters, and had kneaded enough bread to feed a growing family for two generations.

Her hands had planted daffodils and marigolds, and held the shy faces of pansies with gentle fingers. They'd trained morning glories and little children; twisted pin curls, and thrown cold water on fighting cats; bathed babies and scrubbed heads, and waged a lifelong battle with dirt.

On the last day of her life they had held her Bible, made vegetable soup, and shortened a new pair of slacks for Sara. Aristocratic hands, Sara always thought, with long fingers that tapered at the ends.

The family had put gloves on her hands folded in their silent sleep, for Grandma had been ashamed of their tracing of veins and always said that a lady never went out without gloves.

Playful hands

Sara's mother's hands were different, Sara mused. Short, square, and unlike Grandma's, they were busy outside the home, flying over a typewriter and running a calculator as well as they played the piano.

Not good at baking, inept at sewing, and a disaster at handwork, her hands beat fudge to creamy perfection and drew funny pictures that delighted her children. They swung a great miniature golf club and beat time to music.

And her hands were gentle, holding her children, cuddling them, pouring her love into them. Coming home from work after a long day, she always had time to draw them close.

Sadness washed over Sara. *What will my children remember of my hands?* she thought. *I don't have time to make cookies or decorate cakes. Even sewing on a button is impossible these days.*

Caressing hands

But when Sara came home from work at night, she could not get enough of touching her children. The fine silkiness of her young son's hair, the solid roundness of her youngest daughter, just hugging the older girls—her hands had to touch.

But they flew in those minutes, too, slapping together dinner and slinging dirty dishes through suds. Time nipped at her heels. She rushed her boy through his bath and hurried him into his pajamas. When she finally lay down to sleep, it was always with regret. *Hands should comfort,* she often thought. *They should caress and love.*

An unusual noise pulled her from sleep that night, and she made her way through the dark house to the 10-year-old's bed. She found the little girl tossing on a fever-heated pillow and led her, trailing a sheet, into the living room.

Easing down into the high-backed rocker, she settled the long-legged child on her lap and began to rock. Her hands rubbed the hot, thin back. "That feels good, Mama," the little girl whispered. Sara's hands soothed the burning forehead. The two rocked quietly for some minutes before Sara went for fever-reducer and water. Light from the street lamp puddled across the living room floor, and she "walked" the chair toward it until they rocked in its golden glow.

At last the child dozed off, and Sara carried her back to bed. She let her hand rest briefly on the cooling forehead before going to her own room.

"You know what, Mama? There's something funny about your hands," the child said the next day. "When I'm cold, your hands are warm. And when I'm hot—like last night—your hands are always cool."

Then she looked up, obviously asking a serious question. "Don't you think it's funny that your hands are always exactly what I need?"

~ ~ ~

Penny Estes Wheeler wrote this story about herself and her family when she first started working outside of the home. She's rocked a lot of miles since then, most recently rocking her young granddaughter—when she can catch her.

Lest We Forget

Kim Peckham

Let us consider the human brain. This wonderful organ can recall millions of bits of information. Unfortunately, most of them are advertising jingles. The stuff you really want to remember—like where you parked the car at the airport—is gone with the wind.

That's been my experience anyway. When it comes to memory, my mind has a mind of its own. I have come to it on bended knee, begging, "Please, could you find someplace in those billions of neurons to store my telephone calling card number?"

It says, "Sorry, I just used the last of the space for a McDonald's jingle—'Two all beef patties, special sauce, lettuce, cheese, etc.'"

I say, "I don't need to know *that*. I'm a vegetarian!"

To paraphrase the apostle Paul: "Those things I want to remember, I do not."

For example, I wish I could remember people's names. A familiar face will approach me, and I'll desperately ring up my brain. *What's the name of this person who is embracing me like a long-lost relative?*

I can almost hear it suppress a snicker. "I'm not sure I have that file anymore," it giggles. "I think I had to clear it out to make room for your part in the Easter play."

As further proof that our minds are as mischievous as a tent full of Pathfinders, let me mention a little trick they pull on us called "Stop the music." This is where you start singing a song like "Born free, as free as the wind blows. As free as . . ." and suddenly you're humming because you have no idea what words come next. I think most people can sing only two songs clear through from memory: "Do, Lord," and the theme song to the *Beverly Hillbillies*.

Sometimes it seems as though a cheap computer hard drive would do a better job than the standard brain. You could instantly save important facts. Guys could remember the score to every football game. Women could remember every comment anyone ever made about their hair.

Another benefit is that it would take only the press of a button to delete the annoying little memories that brains cling to: for example, that embarrassing moment at your first academy banquet.

"But wait," I hear you saying. "What if you accidentally delete files you need?"

My answer to you is "Ha. That's the least of my worries, because . . . ah . . . Could you repeat the question?"

What I mean is, my brain already deletes everything. It deletes birthdays, anniversaries, the reason I drove to the grocery store.

This isn't so bad if you're a guy, because your wife will remember for you. Solomon forgot to mention that a wife who is more precious than rubies is a wife who can tell you where you left your car keys.

Marriage is a good thing for the forgetful. Lori and I can sometimes remember an important fact if we combine our memories. "What's the name of that restaurant that So-and-so recommended?" I'll ask her. "I think it starts with an 'f.'" This is her clue that the name of the restaurant actually begins with any letter in the alphabet except f, and we work from there.

So what can you do about a declining memory? Deep down, it worries me. What if this forgetfulness continues to creep over the whole mind until I can't even recognize the people I love? It happens.

But you know, even if I forget everything, God remembers. In fact, He remembers me so well that at His return, He will re-create me in every detail—a living, breathing, joyful citizen of the new earth.

Do, Lord, O do remember me.

~ ~ ~

Kim Peckham and his wife, Lori, love remembering the good things they've enjoyed—their courtship, jet skiing, trips to Hawaii, and most recently the birth of their son, Reef Lee.

Finding Dude

Lori Bledsoe, as told to Rhonda Reese

The first time Bart told me about his horse, Dude, I knew their bond had been something special. But I never suspected Dude would bring a wonderful gift to me.

Bart loved all animals, but Dude, the chestnut-colored quarter horse he received when he turned 9, was his favorite. Years later when his dad sold Dude, Bart grieved in secret.

Even before I met and married Bart, I knew about grieving in secret. My dad's job led our family to relocate every year. Deep inside, I wished we could stay in one place where I could have deep, lasting friendships. But I never said anything to my parents. Yet sometimes I wondered if even God could keep track of us.

One summer evening in 1987, as Bart and I glided on our front porch swing, he suddenly asked, "Did I ever tell you that Dude won the World Racking Horse Championship?"

"Rocking horse championship?"

"*Racking,*" Bart corrected, smiling gently. "It's a kind of dancing horses do. Takes lots of training. You use four reins. It's pretty hard." Bart gazed at the pasture. "Dude was the greatest racking horse ever."

"Then why'd you let your dad sell him?" I probed.

"I didn't know he was even thinking about it," Bart explained. "When I was 17, I'd started a short construction job down in Florida. I guess Dad figured I wouldn't be riding anymore, so he sold Dude without even asking me. Running a horse farm means you buy and sell horses all the time.

"I've always wondered if that horse missed me as much as I've missed him. I've never had the heart to try to find him. I couldn't stand knowing if something bad . . ."

Bart's voice trailed off.

Gotta find that horse

After that, few nights passed without Bart mentioning Dude. My heart ached for him, but there was nothing I could do. Then one afternoon while I walked through the pasture, a strange thought came to me. In my heart, a quiet voice said, "Lori, find Dude for Bart."

How absurd! I thought. I knew nothing about horses, certainly not how to find and buy one. That was Bart's department.

The harder I tried to dismiss the thought, the stronger it grew. I dared not mention it to anyone except God. Each day I asked Him to guide me.

One morning, three weeks after that first "find Dude" notion, a new meter reader, Mr. Parker, stopped by while I was working in the garden. We struck up a friendly conversation. When he mentioned he'd once bought a horse from Bart's dad, I interrupted.

"You remember the horse's name?" I asked.

"Sure do," Mr. Parker said. "Dude. Paid $2,500 for him."

I wiped the dirt from my hands and jumped up, barely catching my breath.

"Do you know what happened to him?" I asked.

"Yep. I sold him for a good profit."

"Where's Dude now?" I asked. "I need to find him."

"That'd be impossible," Mr. Parker explained. "I sold that horse years ago. He might even be dead by now."

"But could you . . . would you be willing to try to help me find him?" After I explained the situation, Mr. Parker stared at me for several seconds. Finally, he agreed to join the search for Dude, promising not to say anything to Bart.

Racking, tracking

Each Friday, for almost a year, I phoned Mr. Parker to see if his sleuthing had turned up anything. Each week his answer was the same. "Sorry, nothing yet."

One Friday I called Mr. Parker with another idea. "Could you at least find one of Dude's babies for me?"

"Don't think so," he said, laughing. "Dude was a gelding."

"That's fine," I said. "I'll take a gelding baby."

"You really *do* need help." Mr. Parker explained that geldings are unable to sire. But now he seemed to double his efforts and several weeks later he phoned.

"I found him," he shouted. "I found Dude."

"Where?" I wanted to jump through the phone.

"On a farm in Georgia." Mr. Parker said. "A family bought Dude for their teenage son. But they can't do anything with the horse. In fact, they think Dude's crazy. Maybe dangerous. Bet you could get him back real easy."

Mr. Parker was right. I called the family in Rising Fawn, Georgia, and made arrangements to buy Dude back for $300. I struggled to keep my secret until the weekend. On Friday, I met Bart at the front door after work.

"Will you go for a ride with me?" I asked in my most persuasive voice. "I have a surprise for you."

"Honey," Bart protested, "I'm tired."

"Please, Bart. I've packed a picnic supper. It'll be worth the ride. I promise."

Bart got into the jeep. As I drove, my heart thumped so fast I thought it'd burst as I chatted about family matters.

"Where are we going?" Bart asked after 30 minutes.

"Just a bit farther," I said.

Bart sighed. "Honey, I love you. But I can't believe I let you drag me off."

I didn't defend myself. I'd waited too long to ruin things now. However, by the time I steered off the main highway and onto a gravel road, Bart was so aggravated that he wasn't speaking to me. When I turned from the gravel road to a dirt trail, Bart glared.

Just whistle

"We're here," I said, stopping in front of the third fence post.

"Here where? Lori, have you lost your mind?"

"Stop yelling," I said. "Whistle."

"What?" Bart shouted.

"Whistle," I repeated. "Like you used to . . . for Dude . . . just whistle.

You'll understand in a minute."

"Well . . . I . . . this is crazy," Bart sputtered as he got out of the jeep.

Bart whistled. Nothing happened.

"Oh, please God," I whispered, "don't let this be a mistake."

"Do it again," I prodded.

Bart whistled once more, and suddenly we heard a sound in the distance. What was it? I could barely breathe.

Bart whistled again. Suddenly, over the horizon, a horse came at a gallop. Before I could speak, Bart leapt over the fence.

"Dude!" he yelled, running toward his beloved friend. I watched the blur of horse and husband meet like one of those slow-motion reunion scenes on TV. Bart hopped up on his pal, stroking his mane and patting his neck.

"That horse is crazy"

Immediately a sandy-haired, tobacco-chewing teenage boy and his huffing parents crested the hill.

"Mister!" the boy yelled. "What are you doing? That horse is crazy. Can't nobody do nothin' with 'im."

"No," Bart boomed. "He's not crazy. He's Dude."

To the amazement of everyone, at Bart's soft command to the unbridled horse, Dude threw his head high and began racking. As the horse pranced through the pasture, no one spoke. When Dude finished dancing for joy, Bart slid off of him.

"I want Dude home," he said.

"I know," I said with tears in my eyes. "All the arrangements have been made. We can come back and get him."

"Nope," Bart insisted. "He's coming home tonight."

I phoned my in-laws, and they arrived with a horse trailer. We paid for Dude and headed home.

Bart spent the night in the barn with his old friend. I knew he and Dude had a lot of catching up to do. As I looked out of the bedroom window, the moon cast a warm glow over the farm. I smiled, knowing my husband and I now had a wonderful story to tell our future children and grandchildren.

"Thank You, Lord," I whispered. Then the truth hit me. I'd searched longer for Dude than I'd ever lived in one place. God used the process of finding my husband's beloved horse to renew my trust in the Friend who sticks closer than a brother.

"Thank You, Lord," I whispered again. "Thank You for never losing track of Dude—or me."

~ ~ ~

Lori Bledsoe is a stay-at-home mom taking care of her husband, two daughters, and assorted farm critters.

Rhonda Reese is a freelance writer and frequent contributor to Christian magazines.

Where's Stacy?

La Annette Potter, as told to Helen Heavirland

Where's Stacy?"

The happy banter silenced. Then everyone talked at once.

"She was standing by the fire."

"She asked me for a graham cracker just a few minutes ago."

"The last time I saw her . . ."

Those that weren't talking looked under tables, behind trees.

I questioned that my 3-year-old Stacy would go anyplace, especially in the dark. She never got far from Mama, even at home. Camping among the pines by Jubilee Lake with our church's 11 primary class children and their teachers and families, she'd stuck to me like glue. She'd wanted to go with me minutes before, but I told her, "I'm going to the tent to fix Kristin's bottle. You stay with Mrs. Jones.* OK?" She nodded. "I'll be right back," I promised.

But when I returned, she was gone. I ran back to the tent. No Stacy. Checked the outhouse. No Stacy. I raced back to the campfire and screamed, "Where's Stacy?"

Pandemonium broke loose. Some teachers and parents headed toward the lake, some into the woods. Several searched our tent again. Two looked in and around each car. One leader tried to calm the other children and keep them at the campfire.

I panicked. I *had* to find her! Carrying 11-month-old Kristin on my left hip and grasping my 6-year-old Brittany's hand in my right hand, I hurried toward one campsite, then another. "I have a little girl, 3 years old, wearing pink pants and pink tennis shoes and pink socks. She's been missing for 20 minutes. Can you help me look? Her name is Stacy."

Campers grabbed flashlights and headed into the woods. I rushed on, growing more frantic by the second, screaming a frenzied "Stacy? Stacy?" The further I went, the louder I screamed.

Fruitless search

I groped on. Finally, totally exhausted—physically, mentally, and emotionally—I collapsed in the middle of a narrow road. I turned toward Brittany. On my knees I looked directly into her face. Horror filled her big brown eyes. The utter darkness in my soul overwhelmed me. I'd always been independent. But this time I'd already done everything I could. I had no control over where Stacy was or who had her. *I'm helpless,* I realized. *Totally helpless!*

"God, help me!" I cried aloud.

I grabbed Brittany's hand again, struggled to my feet, and looked around. Notoriously poor at directions, I didn't have the slightest idea where our campsite was. I still don't know how we found it.

Back at camp, the primary leader hugged Brittany close. Another woman took Kristin. Patty, one of the other mothers, hugged me. I grabbed her and hung on like my life depended on it.

Patty urged me to stay at camp so I'd know when someone found Stacy, but I couldn't sit still. So we headed down the road side by side, our arms around each other's waists. "We need to pray," I told Patty. The two of us prayed aloud as we walked. "Dear God, please keep Stacy safe. Please bring her back to us."

My voice rose to a wail. "Stacy! Stacy!" Between my cries we heard others call her name from one direction, then another, then another.

"Please, God, lead someone to her."

We walked every road in the campground. At times Patty literally held me up.

"God," I prayed, "my husband will be devastated if anything has happened to Stacy. Please help someone find her."

Trusting God explicitly seemed reasonable when I'd studied abstract words on paper. But . . . now . . . could I relinquish my lost 3-year-old? How could I release her and trust her to God?

On one of our stops back at camp a state patrolman who was camping with his family arrived at our site. "Children lost in this kind of situation are almost always found nearby," he encouraged.

He searched our tent, opening each sleeping bag and searching behind, under, and around every suitcase or bag. No Stacy. He searched each of the other tents in our camp. After looking in, under, and around each nearby vehicle, he took over organizing the search.

Feeling hopeless

Patty and I kept walking. At home I'd been studying about the battle between Christ and Satan. "God, I know whose side I'm on," I prayed. "You are good. No matter what happens, I will not curse You. I will praise Your name." My words carried more assurance than I felt. Our steps crunched in the darkness. "God," I prayed, "I release Stacy to You. She's been Your gift to us. I want her back. But she's Yours."

Once as we neared our campsite the camp caretaker rushed to the patrolman. Patty and I hurried closer to hear. "All the registered vehicles are here except one. And I saw one car leave just a few minutes ago."

That's the car! Stacy's in it! And she's gone! Images of the horrible things evil people do to children clawed at my mind.

"Chase that car down!" the patrolman barked.

The caretaker spun and sprinted away. "We'll blockade the entrance," the patrolman called after him.

A moment later the caretaker's truck roared, then disappeared into the distance.

"God," I prayed, "help him find her soon. She's Your child. You love her more than I do. Lord, please bring her back safely. Or . . . at least . . . don't let her feel pain. But whatever happens, I will not curse You. I will praise Your name."

Later as we neared camp again the patrolman met us. "What kind of socks was your daughter wearing?"

"Little crew socks."

"There's a sock up the road. Would you come identify it?"

We walked up the road and around a bend. He shone his flashlight toward a small sock crumpled on the pavement. Beside it a dark round spot looked like a pool of blood. I sank to the ground and reached for the sock.

"Don't touch it," the trooper barked. "It's evidence."

Evidence! The word exploded in my mind. *Even the trooper has given up hope.*

175

I pulled back my hand and leaned down close, staring at what might be the last vestige of my daughter. That moment seemed like eternity. The patrolman leaned closer with his flashlight. This sock was white. I sighed with relief. "It's not Stacy's."

For more than an hour Patty and I walked. I thought about my Stacy at the bottom of the lake. I sobbed. I thought about her in the car of strangers. I prayed. I screamed "Stacy? Stacy?" until I was hoarse.

Fighting Satan

Suddenly a thought struck like a bolt of lightning. Much more profound than when God speaks to my mind, it was an almost-audible voice. *The lake. The car. The sock. Satan is creating illusions to take your mind off Me.*

"God, forgive me," I prayed. "You are my Lord. Satan is not going to win. I love You even more than I love Stacy. Whatever happens, I will not curse Your name. I will praise You."

The feeling of utter darkness started to close in again. "Satan," I said through clenched teeth, "in the name of the Lord Jesus Christ, get behind me."

Suddenly I felt awash in calmness. The night was just as black. There was still no real hope. But though my arms ached to hold the precious child I might never see again, peace settled over me. "I relinquish my daughter to You, God," I prayed aloud.

Go worship Me in your tent, the voice whispered.

Worship? I questioned. *Now?*

The voice spoke again clearly. *Go worship Me in your tent.*

We headed back toward camp, and with each step the idea of worshiping God became less a command, more a deep desire of my heart.

When we arrived, the patrolman told me, "We're going to call in the search-and-rescue dogs."

For an instant I started to despair. But I caught myself. *God,* I prayed silently, *You will be glorified.* I turned to Patty. "I have to go by myself to my tent and worship."

Patty looked at me as though I was crazy. "You're not going to go search by yourself, are you?"

"No. I promise. I can't really explain it, but I have to go to my tent and worship."

Inside the tent I knelt. "God, You are mighty . . ."

The soft voice spoke again. *Look in Stacy's sleeping bag one more time.*

Why? I thought. *I've already looked in it several times. Countless others have patted it, shook it, and unzipped and looked in it. Friends and strangers have searched every inch of this tent. And we've screamed her name from right here.*

Look in Stacy's sleeping bag one more time, the voice repeated.

"OK, Lord." I turned around, unzipped Stacy's bag, and turned the top back. Something wiggled. I leaned down closer and patted . . . "She's here!" I screamed at the top of my lungs. I lunged out the tent door. "She's here! She's here!"

They tell me that dozens of searchers converged around me. I didn't notice. Nothing, not even my motherly instinct to cradle my daughter, could quell my other desire. I fell to my knees and worshiped.

Afterword

All those searching rushed to LaAnnette's tent when she started screaming, "She's here!" Naturally everyone tried to figure out what had happened. Shortly, one of the teachers who had searched the area exclaimed, "Look!" She pointed to the ground just outside the tent door.

A man shook his head, dumbfounded. "They weren't there before. I combed this area with my flashlight. I know they weren't there!"

On the ground lay Stacy's shirt and one of her pink tennis shoes.

Stacy was missing for two hours. She has no memory of the events. Searchers (including the patrolman) offered, then discarded, one explanation after another.

"This is the hardest thing I've ever lived through," says LaAnnette, "but—the best. It was the turning point of my life. I know for a fact that God is capable of seeing me through my worst nightmare. There is no fear left."

---

*Name has been changed.

~ ~ ~

Helen Heavirland, from College Place, Washington, writes for many magazines and is the author of the book *Falling for a Lie*. She enjoys reading, encouraging, and bird-watching.

LaAnnette Potter is a wife and mom in Milton-Freewater, Oregon. She leads Beginners Sabbath school and personal ministries at her church and is active in prayer ministry and introducing others to her friend Jesus.

Two Women, One Love

Kay Rizzo

dith's hand shook as she hung up the telephone. The crank calls had come every day for a week. She didn't know how much more she could stand. She picked up the empty teacups and placed them in the sink. *It couldn't be happening again. He'd promised.*

"Who was that?" her friend Cora asked.

Edith's voice trembled. "I don't know. Some woman claiming to be having an affair with Roger."

"Throw him out!" Cora spit. "You vowed you'd throw him out if it happened again."

Edith hesitated. "We've been married 21 years, Cora. They were good years, at least at first. And I do love him." Her eyes pled with her friend to believe her.

"No, Edith. Not many good years. When he wasn't running around on you? Good times—all those times he was passed out cold on the sofa?" The words were hard, but her tone sad and gentle.

"But these could be crank calls. After all, Roger's been working in the oil fields for the last two months."

Cora was a realist. "And sleeping at the nearest sleazy motel, too."

Edith nodded. She had to admit that no matter how remote Roger's assignment might be on the tribal reservation, there was always a small town nearby with a bar and motel handy.

The other woman

Mia's long, blond tresses tangled around her shoulders as she hung up the phone. Her bedside pillow was moist with tears. Roger hadn't returned

179

from another night of drinking. She'd considered tracking him down in one of the two bars in town, but changed her mind. He always warned her that he needed his space. Besides, there was no way a pregnant 14-year-old would blend in with the crowd.

Looking in the mirror, she saw her bloodshot eyes and blotchy skin. "Oh, yeah, you liked having me around before the baby," she murmured. She ran her hand idly across her swelling belly. "It's all your witch of a wife's fault!"

Two days before, Roger had told her that he'd be returning home at the end of the week. He assured her that he'd see she got back home, wherever *that* was. Mia had been following Roger, her wild and crazy Indian, as she called him, from job to job for the last six months. And if she calculated right, she was five months pregnant.

"Doesn't he see?" she talked to her reflection. "I can give him something his old bag of a woman can't."

She remembered Roger, weeping and drunk, lamenting that he'd never had a child. "The desire of my heart was to be a dad, and she denied me that privilege," he'd sobbed, ignoring the sad truth that Edith *couldn't* bear children. Tears had streamed onto his graying stubble.

Confrontation

"So who is she?"

Edith's eyes flashed with fury. "I told you that once more and you were out of here. Who is she?"

"Twenty-one years, darling. Are you going to throw away 21 years together?" Roger begged. "Doesn't your God have something to say about staying with a repentant, unbelieving husband so that his soul might be saved?"

Edith narrowed her gaze; her lips tightened to a thin line. "Don't blaspheme my Savior with your twisted form of Christianity. I have prayed long and hard over this. And while God will never give up on you, He doesn't want me to allow you to destroy my dignity as His daughter again." She picked up her worn leather purse and headed toward the kitchen door. "I'll expect you to be gone before I get home from work."

"But sweetie, I don't want Mia. What would I want with a 14-year-old girl?"

"Fourteen?" Edith shook her head in disgust. "I never want to see you again."

In her old Chevy, Edith struggled to calm her mind. "O Lord, what do You want me to do? How should I feel? Fourteen years old? *A child.* Oh, help me. Help me to know Your will."

Tears streamed down her cheeks and she struggled to see the road. The five miles to the homeless shelter where she volunteered two days a week as a registered nurse clicked quickly by. Like it or not, her heart still loved him—whatever that meant. But she had to make a new life for herself.

Tossed aside

Three more months passed for Roger and his child lover. When Mia's pregnancy was close to full term he tired of her and dumped her on her parents' doorstep. They took one look at her and threw her out. Broken and suicidal, Mia made her way to a shelter operated by a local charity.

They took her in and gave her kitchen work to pay for her keep. One afternoon as she sliced potatoes Mia cut her finger and went to the infirmary. There she met a nurse named Edith. The two hit it off immediately.

Before Mia knew what was happening, she'd told the friendly caregiver her entire life history, beginning with an abusive father right through the abusive relationship with an oil rigger named Roger.

Long before the last of Mia's story tumbled from her lips, Edith made the connection. Her hands trembled and she struggled to breathe. *O Lord,* she prayed, *this isn't fair. Why did You bring her to me? I hate her. I hate her. She destroyed what was left of me . . .*

The girl wrung her hands as the tears flowed. "I don't know what to do. I can't raise this baby."

"There's always adoption," Edith said evenly.

"Yes, except that Roger is Tule Indian. The tribal council won't let a non-Indian adopt my baby." She gently massaged her belly. "As if any Indian family had room for someone else's kid."

Edith, a member of the tribe herself, knew that was true. Most families on the reservation struggled to feed their own flock without adding another hungry mouth. Especially one that was half White.

As the day of the child's birth grew closer, Mia grew frantic. At nights, bitter tears stained Edith's pillow, too. She'd spent a lifetime longing for children of her own. And now here was this girl-child, having his baby, in a way, her baby. Resentment soured her every thought. But try as she might to hate Mia, Edith found herself loving the naive young girl who'd wrangled to be assigned to the clinic so she could be near the kindly nurse.

And her heart broke the day Mia said, "If I had it to do over, I'd become a nurse just like you."

Edith couldn't concentrate all afternoon and that night, struggling to fall asleep, her thoughts were more jumbled than ever. Suddenly, around 3:00 she sat bolt upright in bed. Everything seemed frighteningly simple. For the first time since she'd met her husband's ex-girlfriend, Edith knew what she had to do.

It seemed that only minutes had passed when the phone rang. It was the local hospital telling her that a girl named Mia Strang was in labor and asking for her. Edith threw on jeans and a blouse and raced to the hospital. She arrived in time to coach the frightened young girl through her last hour of labor and was the first to hold the newborn child. Whatever hate or anger or pain she'd felt toward the baby's mother dissolved into an ocean of love toward the tiny boy. If she'd doubted her 3:00 a.m. epiphany earlier, all doubt was gone.

God had given her a second chance. He would bring good out of bad. He would keep His promise that "in all things God works for the good of those who love Him."*

Amazing solution

A day later when Edith checked Mia and her baby out of the hospital, she drove her car to the highway intersection and parked along the side of the road.

"Mia, I have a proposition for you. If you would be comfortable, I would like to take you and little Roger . . ." she choked on the baby's name. But one glance at the sleeping baby strapped in the infant seat behind her reassured her of her decision. "I would like to take you home to live with me. I would like to raise you as a daughter and your son, as my grandson. Of course, I would hope that you would return to school, maybe even college."

The girl's eyes grew wide with disbelief. "Really? You really mean it?"

"Yes, but there are two things you should know before you decide. First, the father of your baby was my husband."

Mia's jaw dropped. Her eyes filled with fear. She turned around and shielded her son with one hand as if afraid Edith would strike out at her or her child.

"Yes," Edith said softly. "I'm the woman, the wife, you harassed with those phone calls. But I have forgiven both you and my husband long ago."

"B-b-b-but how? I don't understand. How can you forgive me? I hate Roger for what he did to me. I'll never forgive him for abandoning me or our child."

Edith's eyes were warm with compassion. "That's the second thing I want you to know about coming to live with me. The One who made it possible for me to forgive is Jesus Christ. He lives in my home. If you come to live there, too, you'll need to come to terms with Him. Can you do that?"

The girl thought for a moment. "I'll try. I really will try."

Edith gently patted her hand, then eased the car out onto the highway toward her tiny, two-bedroom home on the outskirts of the reservation. "Don't worry. God will do it all," she said. "I promise." They drove on in companionable silence. As they neared the local ice-cream parlor, Edith asked, "How about a nice big milkshake before we leave town?"

Mia broke into a big smile. For the first time since they'd met, her young eyes sparkled with hope and joy and promise.

Epilogue

The facts in this story are true. Only the names and location has been changed. It wasn't long before Edith's attitude of love and forgiveness spilled over into Mia's life, and she gave her heart to the Savior.

She did go back to school. She has a four-year nurses' degree and is working in a local hospital. Little Roger started school last year. He loves Bible stories, especially the ones about Jesus. As for Edith, her once broken heart is bubbling over with love. She's been granted the daughter she never had and a grandson more marvelous than she could have imagined. Her life is filled with receiving hugs and kisses, and making oatmeal cookies.

The child's father is currently serving time in the state of Nevada for accosting a police officer during a bar room brawl. And each night, at bedtime, Edith, Mia, and little Roger pray for the man whose sins brought them together.

If you were to meet Edith today she would tell you, "All things do work together for good—even your worst nightmares—to those who love God and are called according to His purpose."

---

*Romans 8:28

~ ~ ~

Kay Rizzo is a popular retreat speaker that keeps 'em laughing with her commonsense humor. She and her husband, Richard, live in California, and have two daughters and two granddaughters.

I Choose Praise

Cecily Daly

I rolled over, opened my eyes, and drew my first conscious breath. *Today is my challenge* was my first thought. Through the window I saw fleecy clouds, a clear blue sky, and the morning sun. Reassured of God's love and power, I felt strengthened.

Father, I need Your wisdom and strength to help me cope with yesterday's unfinished business. Take away my anxiety and let me praise Your name.

The trills and crescendo of a cockatiel's lighthearted melody spoke to me. By the time it finished its morning serenade my thoughts had changed, for the bird's message was clear.

Every person has a song to sing. So sing!
Whether you are heard or not, do your best.
Sing in the light. Sing in the darkness.
Whether free from difficulties or caged by problems,
Sing!
Don't fret and worry about things you cannot change.
Trust God, and praise His name—and sing!
Someone needs to hear your song, so sing.

Such was the lesson the cockatiel taught me, and I recalled many unexpected answers to prayer. *Yes, just for today,* I thought, *I will praise God and give Him the glory.* Feeling comfortable about my promise, I walked into the business office with fresh confidence, collected my paycheck, and took it home.

Surprise

My paycheck was not just short; it was totally inadequate. How would

I work with it? I shuffled thoughts a hundred times before I remembered my promise: *today is a day of praise.* Surrender was quick; my decision final. I would simply drop the check in the collection plate at church, claim a promise, and praise the Lord.

So I addressed a tithe envelope, endorsed the check, placed both in my Bible, then knelt to ask for help. "Each time you kneel to pray, you ask," I seemed to hear. "Why can't you just praise God? Try Him for yourself and see what happens."

Suddenly I felt sick and tired asking for favors. Subdued, I whispered, "I am just going to praise the Lord. God will have to solve my problem." I bowed my head and thanked Him for everything I could remember. I felt happy and peaceful.

I returned to the business office to discuss my paycheck situation. I didn't ask any favors or suggest solutions, but God worked it out, leaving me open-eyed with astonishment. I left the office lighthearted and thankful. I had taken the psalmist's advice, sang a new song, and learned the lesson that God is pleased with "praise, the highest form of prayer."

Five steps to perfect praise

1. Recall the occasion of your highest praise.
2. Ponder if your offerings to Him reflect your gratitude.
3. Declare a "praise day" in which you will neither petition nor intercede.
4. Daily set aside five to 10 minutes for a praise break.
5. Notice the positive changes your daily praise break makes in your life.

~ ~ ~

Cecily Daly, Ph.D., is an associate professor in the Department of English and Communications at Oakwood College, Huntsville, Alabama. A freelance writer and youth worker whose hobbies include gardening, reading, and listening to music, she is the mother of two daughters.

Christmas Alone?

Elizabeth Boyd

It's December 25, and I slowly open one eye and allow myself a moment of self-pity.

I'm single. There's nobody to snuggle with on Christmas morning, no children creeping out of bed to see what's under the tree. In years past the fragrance of pumpkin pie and sweet potato casserole promised a traditional New England Christmas dinner. But not this year.

I glance around my bedroom and see ribbons of sunlight slanting through the east window. With its old-fashioned red wallpaper, white ruffled curtains, and two white alpaca fur rugs atop the red carpet, it's almost a "Christmas room." An oil painting of a thawing stream and winter trees hangs above the mantel. Well, at least the picture has snow. I smile as my eyes find the pine boughs and red-berried holly atop the bedroom mantel. There's a red candle, too.

House full of joy

Was it only last Sunday that this house was full of laughter? An eighth grader with a blond ponytail had decorated this mantel with her friend Allison. They cut the holly themselves from the big bush under the picture window. They and their friends tramped through the woods snipping pine boughs and fir branches. Cheryl and Christina made a wreath for the front door and decorated the banister with a streamer of green pine dotted with more holly berries.

Tall, graceful Debbie, working alone on the mantel in the living room, called, "Miss Elizabeth, come see! Do you have any Christmas balls or anything? This arrangement needs something to balance it with the red candle."

Scents of savory loaf and potatoes wafted through the house from the big kitchen.

Sarah and my namesake, Elizabeth, came up to the attic where I was digging out the tree ornaments. "What does baking powder do?" they asked, a blush on their pretty faces.

"Cooks put it in muffins and stuff to make it rise," I answered. "Why?"

"Well, I guess it'll be OK then," Elizabeth said. "We thought 't-s-p' meant tablespoon, so we put three tablespoons of baking powder in the muffin batter instead of three teaspoons!"

"Maybe they'll puff up and be all over the oven," Sarah groaned. "And it's too late to make another batch. I guess we'll just have to eat them."

I followed the girls into the kitchen. The sun was shining through the big bay window on the south side of the house. The sun slants low during the short days of winter in Maine, but I like it. It shines onto the red checkered tablecloth that covers the old, round wooden table. It always fades the fabric, but sunshine makes the kitchen seem so cheerful.

The embers of a fire lingered in the Franklin stove, and the room was abuzz with activity. The muffin girls occupied the bake center. The salad girls were cutting celery sticks and stuffing them with cream cheese. The candy girls were grinding fresh cranberries, apples, and oranges with the old meat grinder that belonged to my grandmother.

Beth, Sharon, and Tiffany were busy in the dining room. "Which tablecloth can we use, Miss Elizabeth?"

"Oh, any of them."

"Even the white linen one?" Sharon questioned.

"Yes. Someone has already spilled cranberry juice on it, and I know what to do about it. You dip it in boiling water and the stain comes right out!"

"Can we use the glasses with long stems?" Tiffany asked.

"Oh, yes. I know you girls will be especially careful. Those glasses belonged to my grandmother, but I'd rather take a chance that they'll survive a house full of young ladies than keep them in the glass cabinet for my own grandchildren, which I'll never have. Make the table beautiful! Your mothers will appreciate it when they join us in a couple of hours."

Dress-up

"Oh, Miss Elizabeth," sighed my namesake, "we didn't bring anything but jeans with us. With the food so good and the house so beautiful, we need beautiful clothes."

I smiled to myself. Eighteen years ago her mother, Penny, was one of the young women who'd helped decorate my old farmhouse for Christmas. She'd said the same thing. I wondered if Elizabeth knew the story from her mother.

"Go ahead," I laughed. "You can play dress-up. The closet is open. Try on whatever makes you happy. The summer clothes are in the closet at the top of the stairs."

Within minutes clothes were strewn all over the red upstairs bedroom and the blue downstairs bedroom as the girls tried on and discarded outfit after outfit. They emerged from the bedrooms attired in swirling dresses, business suits, and bathing suits with beach jackets, just in time to entertain their mothers.

I glanced at their bare feet—every one of them. How is it that a 13-year-old's feet are full size before the rest of her body? Their feet were all too large for my size 6 heels, while their bodies were too small for my dresses. But when their feet were under the table no one would know.

Sarah and Elizabeth exchanged glances as they bit into the beautiful blueberry muffins. They didn't take a second bite, and neither did anyone else! We now know that three tablespoons of baking powder tastes like three tablespoons of salt! Even butter wouldn't make them go down.

For the entertainment my young guests insisted on a command performance talent show. ". . . and you, Miss Elizabeth, will sing for us 'Silent Night,'" Anna said with her winsome smile.

"Oh, I'd love to," I answered, "but I sing only harmony. Maybe your mother and I could sing a duet."

"Oh, that's fine. But you gotta' do your part," Anna teased.

After the dinner and conversation and entertainment were over, the girls cleared the table, put the dishes in the dishwasher, and even picked up the clothes that lay in colorful puddles about the bedrooms. With hugs and smiles, mothers and daughters went into the December night, leaving me with a heart full of joy and happy memories.

But that was five days ago.

Today is Christmas.

The girls and their mothers are busy unwrapping presents under their own trees. I'm lying alone in my queen-sized bed in an empty house.

I bounce out of bed and head for the shower. Maybe my Christmas was five days ago. Who says it has to be on December 25, anyway!

~ ~ ~

For a four-year period Elizabeth Boyd left teaching and physical therapy, and traveling alone with a fifth wheeler and one-ton truck, did relief work in U.S.A. facilities. Her most precious moments are watching sunrises with Jesus near her farmhouse in Harpswell, Maine.

Surprise Me

Christmas is just around the corner—that wonderful time of year when families get together to exchange both gifts and the flu virus. I hope I didn't cause any of you to panic as you realize that you still have 37 names to go on your Christmas list, and the only way you can finish shopping on time is to quit your day job and park your camper at the mall.

Christmas used to be simpler. The toughest thing about shopping was finding some shiny apples for the children's stockings.

If you want to make a gift of an apple these days, it better have 128 megs of RAM and a color printer. Modern kids come up with wish lists that bear a striking resemblance to the inventory records of Toys 'R' Us.

But that's what makes it easy to shop for kids—they're not shy about telling you what they want, sometimes even renting billboards along your route to work, or making impassioned speeches about the critical role of new in-line skates to their future welfare and self-esteem.

Adults are more cagey. Especially mothers, who will say things such as, "You don't have to buy me anything this year. It's enough that you're spending Christmas with me. What more can I ask for than the privilege of cooking for you and cleaning up after you?"

If you have someone like this on your gift list—someone who is not forthcoming with any ideas—let me suggest an item I saw in the Sharper Image catalog. I refer to the Electric Tongue Cleaner, priced at a reasonable $30, with a long, slim design that "makes it easy to clean the important area far back on your tongue." (Battery not included.)

The next time you ask the recipient of this gift what they want for Christmas, I guarantee you will get answers!

Actually, my own wife will not tell me what she wants for Christmas. This, no doubt, is a result of my deeply held belief that the best gifts are a surprise.

In our early years of marriage Lori would say, "I'd love to have a new vacuum cleaner for Christmas."

And I would respond, "Well, now I can't get that for you, because it wouldn't be a surprise."

Soon Lori learned to ask me only for things she doesn't want. "I could sure use another pair of Isotoner gloves," she'll say.

I know I'm not the only one who values the element of surprise. I'm thinking of Melody, who married into a family whose chief pre-holiday amusement involves guessing what gifts are coming their way. They are not above shaking presents, sleuthing through closets, or peeking into shopping bags.

Every time one of her purchases is discovered, though, Melanie insists on returning it to the store, often with an in-law close behind saying, "But I really *wanted* that." One year she had to buy a new present three times for the same relative.

In my mind, surprising gifts contain elements of the divine. When we bring our desires to our heavenly Father, He often asserts His privilege to surprise us—to give us something better than we asked for. Or to deliver what we asked for in an unexpected way.

If you want someone who will simply deliver the items on your wish list, then you're not looking for God. You're looking for Santa Claus.

~ ~ ~

Kim Peckham and his wife, Lori, have a brand-new reason to celebrate Christmas. Now they enjoy the holiday through the eyes of their young son, Reef.

Christmas Miracle

*Dr. Joseph A. MacDougall,
as told to Douglas How*

Finally, one day that December I had to tell her. Medically, we were beaten. The decision lay with God.

She took it quietly, lying there, wasting away, only 23 and the mother of a year-old child.

Eleanor Munro* was a devout, courageous woman. She had red hair and had probably been rather pretty, but it was hard to tell anymore. She was so near to death from tuberculosis.

She knew it now. She accepted it, and she asked for just one thing.

"If I'm still alive on Christmas Eve," she said slowly, "I would like your promise that I can go home for Christmas."

It disturbed me. I knew she shouldn't go. The lower lobe of her right lung had a growing tubercular cavity in it an inch in diameter. She had what doctors call open TB and could spread the germs by coughing.

The promise

But I made the promise. Frankly, I did so because I was sure she'd be dead before Christmas. In the circumstances, it seemed little enough to do. And if I hadn't made it, I wouldn't be telling this story.

Eleanor's husband had the disease when he returned from overseas service in World War II. Before it was detected and checked, they married. She caught the disease, and had little immunity against it. It came on so fast and lodged in such a difficult place, it confounded every doctor who tried to help her.

To have a tubercular cavity in the lower lobe is rare. When they took her to the provincial sanatorium in Kentville, it became obvious that the

193

main problem was how to get at it. If it had been in the upper lobe, they could have performed an operation that involves taking out some of the upper ribs to collapse the lobe, and put that area of the lung at rest.

Unfortunately, this couldn't be used for the lower lobe. It would have meant removing some of the lower ribs, which her body needed for support. And in any case, it probably would not collapse the cavity.

With that ruled out, they tried a process that uses needles to pump in air to force collapse of the lung through pressure. Although the doctors made several attempts, this didn't work because previous bouts of pleurisy had stuck her lung to her chest wall and the air couldn't circulate.

Finally they considered a rare surgical procedure—taking out the entire lung. But they rejected it because Eleanor was too sick to withstand surgery, and steadily getting worse.

Their alternatives exhausted, they reluctantly listed her as a hopeless case and sent her back to her home hospital in Antigonish.

I was 31, and I hadn't been there very long. At St. Martha's Hospital I provided an anesthesia service and looked after a small TB annex, a place for about 40 patients, most of them with little or no hope of cure.

That's how Eleanor Munro came to be my patient in 1947. She had weighed 125 pounds but was down to 87 the first time I saw her. Her fever was high, fluctuating between 101 and 103 degrees. She was, and looked, very toxic.

But she could still smile, I'll always remember. If you did her the slightest kindness, she'd smile.

Maybe that encouraged me; I don't know. But I did know that I had to try to help her.

I first called a top expert in Montreal on the use of a new drug called streptomycin. He told me the drug wasn't available. When I described the case, he said he would advise against its use anyway.

I then phoned a doctor in New York who was experimenting with a procedure of injecting needles into the peritoneal cavity to force in air and push the diaphragm up against the lung. If we could get pressure against that lower lobe, we could hope to force the TB cavity shut.

If we could do that, nature would have a chance to close and heal the cavity by letting the sides grow together.

At the hospital we considered the risks and decided we had to face them. We operated to pump air into Eleanor's peritoneal cavity.

But it nearly killed her. It was obvious that the amount of air she could tolerate could in no way help. Every doctor in the room agreed we shouldn't try a second time. We were licked.

I told her that medical science had gone as far as it could go. As I explained why in detail, she listened with quiet dignity and an amazing resignation. I told her that her Creator had the final verdict. It might not be what either of us wanted, but it would be the best for her under the circumstances.

She nodded, and then exacted from me that promise.

Amazingly, she was still alive on Christmas Eve, though just barely. But she held me to my promise, and with renewed doubts, I kept it. I told her not to hold her child and to wear a surgical mask if she was talking to anyone but her husband. His own case had given him immunity.

She promised, and off she went by ambulance, wearing that smile I can't forget.

She came back to St. Martha's late on Christmas Day, and she kept ebbing.

No one could have watched her struggle without being deeply moved. Every day her condition grew just a bit worse, yet every day she clung to life.

Toward the end of February, she was down to 80 pounds; she couldn't eat—and new complications set in. She became nauseated and began to vomit even without food in her stomach.

I was stumped. I called in a senior medical consultant, and when he examined her, he was stumped too. But with a grin, almost jokingly, he asked me if I thought she could be pregnant.

The suggestion seemed ridiculous. Everything I knew about medical science added up to one conclusion: she was so ill, so weak, she couldn't possibly have conceived. Her body just wasn't up to it. Nevertheless, I did a pregnancy test. To my astonishment, it was positive. On the very outer frontier of life itself, she now bore a second life within her. It was as close to the impossible as you're ever likely to get, but it was true.

When I told her, she smiled and faintly blushed.

Legally and medically, we could have taken that child through abortion because it periled a life that was already in jeopardy. But we didn't do it. The patient and her husband were against it. We doctors at St. Martha's were against it, not only on religious grounds, but because we were certain the operation would kill her. Besides, she was so far gone that we were sure her body would reject the child anyway.

So we fed her intravenously and watched her fight to sustain two lives in a body in which only some remarkable strength of character or divine intervention had allowed her to sustain even one.

The struggle went on for weeks, and never once did we alter our conviction that she was dying. But she simply refused to die. And she kept her child.

Saved by her baby

And then an incredible thing began to happen. By late March I was confounded to find her temperature beginning to go down. For the first time, we noted some improvement in her condition. She began to eat and to gain weight.

A chest X-ray showed that the growth of the TB cavity had stopped. Soon after, another X-ray showed that her diaphragm was pushing up against the lower lobe of her diseased lung to make room for the child she bore.

Nature was doing what we'd failed to do—it was pressing the sides of that deadly hole together. The child was saving the mother!

The child did save her. By the time it was born, a normal, healthy baby, the TB cavity was closed.

Eleanor was remarkably better, so much so that we let her go home for good within a few months. Her smile had never been brighter.

I still remember with delight the Christmas cards she sent me for years. They were just ordinary cards, with the usual printed greetings. But to me, they were like monuments to a miracle of Christmas.

~ ~ ~

Douglas How has been writing for more than 60 years. A war and parliamentary correspondent, he's also worked on the editorial staff of *Time* and *Reader's Digest,* and published six books. His small town of St. Andrews, New Brunswick, Canada, has named him their community poet.

Wings for Christmas

Sylvia Schappell, as told to her sister, Elaine Dodd

It was Christmas Eve. Dream-perfect greeting-card scenes flowed by as I drove alone through a frozen Wisconsin landscape. After traveling more than an hour, I was almost home. But my thoughts crackled as bitterly as the −50°F windchill outside the car.

Home—what a joke!

This was my second Christmas hundreds of miles away from family and friends. Only Angel, my plush-coated white cat, was waiting for me in the apartment. I'd been betrayed by my roommate, the woman who'd persuaded me to move here after my divorce. She'd taken over my life, pretending to help because I needed a wheelchair. I always thought I was a good judge of character, but months later I discovered she was an experienced con artist who'd been using my credit cards and stealing from my safety deposit box.

With her trial pending, my testimony would help put her in prison again. In the meantime my nerves were deteriorating, both physically and emotionally. I hated feeling so empty and devastated.

I've been naturally cheerful all my life. Even though doctors had predicted I'd never walk again after a spinal injury at age 19, I *had* walked! For more than 20 years. But my limp had grown progressively worse until I needed a cane, then a walker, and eventually a wheelchair for long distances. Then came my divorce and a move to another state. Finally I could no longer stand and relied upon my arms to hoist my body from bed to chair to tub, etc. Even so, my attitude had always been Who wants to hear complaints?

"How does Sylvia manage?" someone asked my elderly father in California.

"With a smile!" he replied. He was right. Smiling requires less effort than frowning.

Serious problems

But now I was losing the use of my right arm. Unpaid bills were mounting—most of which my ex-roommate had incurred. My ancient Buick with the wheelchair carrier top needed constant maintenance. I had no income. This time I was overwhelmed. My usually strong faith in God had become as weak as my legs! Did He even exist?

Just as I entered the bridge over Lake Butte des Morts, I heard a thunk! then a scratching sound, and saw some white feathers near the top of my car window. "Oh, no, I've hit a seagull!" I wailed.

I love animals and couldn't bear the thought of a dead bird caught in my wheelchair topper. But there was no place to stop, so I drove on. Suddenly a tune that I'd learned as a child at church came to mind, and I began singing, "God sees the little sparrow fall. It meets His tender view. If God so loves the little bird, I know He loves me too."

After a few miles I saw a place to pull off the road—a used-car lot— but now what could I do? I had no idea. Helpless to stand, I could never disentangle the poor bird. As I sat in the dark feeling worthless, another vehicle pulled into the lot. Its interior lights snapped on, and I could see a young man studying a map.

I began tapping my horn, but he showed no reaction. I honked louder and longer. Still no response. "Well, are you *deaf?*" I muttered in irritation as I began flashing my lights on and off. Finally he glanced up, sat a moment, then got out and approached my car. As I opened my door he handed me a pad and pencil. To my chagrin, written on the pad were the words "I can't hear. May I help you?"

Great, golden eyes

Taking the pad, I wrote, "*I can't walk, but look—*" and I pointed upward. He raised his eyes and sprang back, startled. At that moment the bird struggled, its head dropped over the front of my windshield, and two great, round, golden eyes stared into mine. It was a snowy owl. Still alive!

After retrieving a long-handled ice scraper from his car, the young man ever-so-gently pushed the owl out from under my wheelchair carrier.

The stunned creature scrambled to perch on my open door, then hopped to the ground, gathering its wits for a few moments. Hardly daring to breathe, we watched as it spread its wings to a magnificent five-foot span, lifted, circled, and sailed silently back across the lake.

Together we gazed in wonder as the majestic white image grew smaller and smaller, slowly disappearing into frigid blackness. Then my good Samaritan turned to me, and in thickly pronounced syllables, he broke the enchanted hush. "Merry Christmas!"

As we drove away from each other, my spirits soaring like the owl's wings, I exclaimed aloud, "He's alive. Jesus really is alive!"

~ ~ ~

Sylvia Schappell, at the time of this writing, lived in Wisconsin with her cat, Angel, and her roommate, Simon the Senegal parrot. She has a son and daughter and five grandchildren.

Elaine Dodd, retired from *It Is Written* telecast, lives in California with her husband. They have three children and seven grandchildren.

Author Index

Topic Index